12

Past, Present
and Future

Best wishes

David wells

K

Past, Present and Future

What your Past Lives Tell You about Yourself

DAVID WELLS

HAY HOUSE

Australia • Canada • Hong Kong • India
South Africa • United Kingdom • United States

First published and distributed in the United Kingdom by:
Hay House UK Ltd, 292B Kensal Rd, London W10 5BE. Tel.: (44) 20 8962 1230;
Fax: (44) 20 8962 1239. www.hayhouse.co.uk

Published and distributed in the United States of America by:
Hay House, Inc., PO Box 5100, Carlsbad, CA 92018-5100. Tel.: (1) 760 431 7695 or
(800) 654 5126; Fax: (1) 760 431 6948 or (800) 650 5115. www.hayhouse.com

Published and distributed in Australia by:
Hay House Australia Ltd, 18/36 Ralph St, Alexandria NSW 2015. Tel.: (61) 2 9669
4299; Fax: (61) 2 9669 4144. www.hayhouse.com.au

Published and distributed in the Republic of South Africa by:
Hay House SA (Pty), Ltd, PO Box 990, Witkoppen 2068. Tel./Fax: (27) 11 467 8904.
www.hayhouse.co.za

Published and distributed in India by:
Hay House Publishers India, Muskaan Complex, Plot No. 3, B-2, Vasant Kunj, New
Delhi – 110 070. Tel.: (91) 11 41761620; Fax: (91) 11 41761630.
www.hayhouse.co.in

Distributed in Canada by:
Raincoast, 9050 Shaughnessy St, Vancouver, BC V6P 6E5. Tel.: (1) 604 323 7100;
Fax: (1) 604 323 2600

A catalogue record for this book is available from the British Library.

ISBN 978-1-4019-1564-3

Printed and bound in Great Britain by TJ International, Padstow, Cornwall.

041131026

This book is dedicated to my mum and my sister.

Without their unconditional love my lives would not

have been the same.

Contents

Preface   ix

Acknowledgements   xi

Chapter 1: First steps   1

Chapter 2: The Akashic records   29

Chapter 3: One step at a time   45

Chapter 4: Challenging lives   67

Chapter 5: Courageous lives   81

Chapter 6: Peace   91

Chapter 7: Soul detective   105

Chapter 8: Silence and contemplation   123

Chapter 9: Sudden change   135

Chapter 10: Magical or mythical?   143

Chapter 11: Can you move forward in time?   159

Chapter 12: Past lives and astrology   171

Chapter 13: What now?   199

Appendix: Locating the nodes of the moon   203

Reading and resources   207

Preface

When *David Wells' Complete Guide to Developing your Psychic Skills* was published I received many e-mails and letters, and one thing that struck me among them all was the references to real life, to people applying the exercises and putting their unfolding awareness to practical use.

I firmly believe that our psychic and intuitive gifts are about day-to-day life. They are about making changes to bring us a better life, a life we are happy living, and nothing I have found can make as many profound changes as past-life regression. This is a way for your soul to talk to you and to let you know what it has been through, and for you to tap into the lessons it has to offer and the gifts just waiting for you to use them.

There is great value in consulting your astrologer once a year or in times of need; by all means see a medium if you have lost someone dear to you and need the reassurance that they are still around, and of course go to a Tarot reader if it's what you want to do. I do some of those things myself. Remember, though, that afterwards it's down to you to get on with living the life you're in here and now. But you can always surpass your wildest dreams if you apply yourself!

'Life goes on' is a saying you will hear often, but in those three words lie the lessons of eternity. Life does go on – we incarnate, die, reincarnate, over and over, each lifetime full of lessons to give and receive.

Every day is a day filled with opportunity. If you seize it you can push your life on faster than you could ever have imagined. If you invest some time and effort in your soul and your mind, you can go wherever you want to go and do whatever you want to do, but first find your skills, find your strengths and work on those weaknesses.

I promise you I will always show you practical uses for your magical gifts.

David Wells

Acknowledgements

So many people help you in so many ways when you write a book. Your mates back off and give you space, your colleagues ask how it's going and ply you with chocolate cake when you almost faint at the nothingness you've achieved so far, and your family say zilch, knowing that even in school you always panicked and did it anyway. Here are the names:

Lee Fadden, Matthew Cave, Jarvis Cresdee, Diane Carter, Wayne Hamilton, Mark Symonds, Jenni Shell, Jenny Greentree and Norie Miles. For stepping back.

Yvette Fielding, Karl Beattie and Ciarán O'Keeffe for cake and sympathy.

Hay House for advice and understanding.

My mum and my sister for their quiet support.

To all I offer my thanks, and whether you butted out or butted in, the fact you were there is what is important.

And finally my dad, never far from my heart.

CHAPTER 1

FIRST STEPS

The smell of the animals was strong, stronger than anything I had ever smelled before. I could see the straw on the floor and the blood that was mixed with it was as cold as my mother's heart when she handed me over to a woodsman and his wife. In that instant I knew it all, the whole of the universe was inside my head, and then as swiftly as it was there it was gone.

Looking through the eyes of a baby is an interesting experience. You see lots of faces peering at you, some with concern and some with disdain, some with love and some with anything but, and it's odd how you know what they are thinking even though you can't talk...

This is how one of my past-life regressions began, a vivid journey full of drama and intrigue, of comfort and camaraderie, in fact the whole gambit of human emotions unfolding in the space of an hour or so – but was it just a story from too many childhood books or adult experiences masquerading as theatre of the mind? That's why you picked this book up, isn't it? To find out if you really have lived before or if you're making it all up.

Nobody can make that decision for you – you have to take the test, see what you can find and work out how relevant it is to your life right now and how it can help you achieve the life you're yet to have.

One thing is for sure – once you embark upon this journey into the depths of your soul memories you will find drama, intrigue and ultimately comfort all of your own.

So what is past-life regression?

Modern life doesn't seem to fit with some of us; we resonate to a different time in space or to a totally different geographical area. Some of the people we meet seem to be familiar before they even open their mouth. Why does this happen? You might suggest that things you learned in school influence where you feel more at home or that a jumble of non-verbal language makes us react to someone in a certain way. Or it may be that past lives go some way towards explaining it. It's up to you to decide and you alone. There is no absolute proof either way – not in the here and now, anyway, and it could be argued that when you do eventually find out for sure you're in no position to let anyone back here know about it!

What I can definitely say is that the first regression I ever had quite literally changed my life. It took me to ancient Greece, a country I adore, but at the time I knew little about. I hadn't been there at the time and whilst I had been taught some Greek history at school, it hadn't particularly stuck in my mind. To be honest, I had rather been hoping for ancient Egypt when I had taken that first step into the world of past lives – and to this date it's not a period I have ever landed in, but I am holding out for it and one day I am sure it will happen. It's funny how you can ask to go to a place in time you feel you have been to before, but if it's more important that you see something else you just don't get it.

A past-life regression, then, is the process of going back into the memory of a former life, a time when you had a totally different personality, face, body and place to live and love in. The stories you experience will all be different, but they will eventually reveal a theme, a way of being that you are still working on today, and once you establish that, you can move through what ails you and embrace the aims you have – sometimes from centuries ago.

A regression reminds you of who you were and can therefore shed some light on who you can be. That's the real deal with past-life regression – it's not just a way of getting great stories to tell your dinner guests, it's something you can work with to understand yourself and your motivation and come up with a plan to stop repeating the same mistakes and begin to build on all the knowledge you have accrued and the experiences you have had.

Body, soul and spirit

So, what are you made up of? You have a physical body that you can see, and even if you sometimes fall out with it, it's yours for this lifetime. Controlling that body is your conscious mind, the bit that moves you along, catches up on the gossip with your mates, remembers Aunty Jenny's birthday and looks forward to two weeks in Malaga at the end of August.

Then you have your soul. It's not really visible, but you know it's there because you can feel something motivating you, talking to you inside your head and making suggestions whenever it can get through all that chatter about shoes, handbags and gearboxes. This part of you remembers everything you have ever said or done – ever, ever, ever, yes, for hundreds of years or more. We will call it the subconscious mind. (Don't be fooled into thinking the subconscious mind comes under the rule of the conscious mind, by the way. It's the most powerful of all and working with it can bring about many changes in your physical and spiritual life.)

The spirit concludes the gang of three. This connects to your soul – it's a bit like one of those poles that goes from the dodgem car to the energy grid above the bit that makes it move. Not literally, of course – that would cause havoc on the Underground! It has extra information, but you do need to put some effort in to access it. Here you get help from spirit guides, dreams and just knowing. It's your universal mind, if you like, the one that knows the most of all.

The way we recall our past lives, as well as what happened last week, is different for all of us. I tend to get the all-singing all-dancing Hollywood version full of colour and emotion, some people just know what to say next and others get very simple images that mean something to them, something they can translate into events. It really doesn't matter how you do it as long as it works for you, but try to use all your senses – all six of them – and don't get huffy if your mate can do it so much better than you can. Chances are, they will be so wrapped up in the amateur dramatics that they will miss something really important. It's swings and roundabouts, so accept the gifts you're given the way you're given them. How much simpler life would be if we all did that!

Why bother? What's the point of it all?

There isn't one point, there are many, and as many as I can think of will be covered in this book, but a great starting place is the word 'karma'.

We all have it and most of us automatically think it's not such a good thing – bad karma seems to be flavour of the century for us humans. Karma needn't be challenging, though. There is good karma, and even the stuff you might call bad is there for a reason and if you change your attitude towards it you will be able to negate it, to work with it and to blend it seamlessly into advancing your soul and spiritual growth.

Karma is a vast subject with many threads and that's a good way to think of it in relation to your past lives. There are threads from your soul memory that have to be taken up and followed to enable you to come to the end and find out how the story turns out. Then you can weave a new piece of cloth for yourself and begin again.

For every action there is a reaction. It's a simple balancing act: you do good, you get good; you do wrong, you get to see what that feels like – and remember, this goes on throughout the centuries, so don't expect it all to come to you this week!

When I was training I remember questioning karma – not in any negative way, just wondering how it truly worked – then one day I accidentally scraped a car in a car park. It was just a little bump, but leaving my address on the windscreen didn't seem enough. Still, I just did that and drove off. They never got in touch, so maybe the note blew off, or maybe it rained ... and then just a few weeks later someone scratched my car and did just drive off – karma or coincidence?

Karma involves much more than mere objects, of course. It's usually about your relationships with those around you and the emotional responses and deeds resulting from those experiences. 'Karma' will be a word you will see a lot as the past lives described in this book are analysed.

Who were you?

So, who are you likely to have been? You may have been black, white, olive and all points in between, male or female, maybe not so sure either way, blue-eyed, brown-eyed, blonde, black or red-headed, rich or poor – you get the point.

Could you have been famous? I call this 'the Cleopatra question', because it's often the character people ask me if I have met – why, I don't know! Not as many famous past lives come to light during regression as those who wish to denigrate past-life work would have you believe. They are very rare, and to be honest, what if someone was famous? I bet their problems were greater than most and therefore the lessons learned would have been greater too. And even if you *were* king of the world once, you're not now. Remember, past-life regression is about the here and now. That's where you use your strengths and deal with your weaknesses.

There is no general thread in the way you look throughout the ages and the same goes for geography – you could have experienced lives throughout the world. But what does seem to occur a lot is that the same people surround you, which raises the question why.

Soul groups

Remember those people you just seem to get on with from day one? They come into your life and they are friends or lovers from the word go. Of course, there are those who stir the exact opposite reaction in you – you don't like them around you and have no earthly reason why not. And don't forget some people will have extreme reactions to you and you may not know why. Sometimes family members may seem so far removed from your way of thinking it's almost comical, and yet there may be a woman in your life who is more like a sister to you than your real sister – the possibilities are endless.

Imagine the greater understanding you would have if you knew which life all these people were part of, what karma you shared and just how you should proceed to work it out. It is possible to recognize these soul groups, the people who have travelled with you through time and space to be here and now and to be part of your future until it's time to move away, having learned as much as you can from each other.

'My soul mate' is one of those misunderstood phrases that people use when they find a partner they are totally committed to; a better expression would be 'one of my soul mates'. You have many, but timing has brought this one to you right now. The reason why you feel so close can be discovered through a past-life regression and in many ways can make that relationship more intense – imagine finding out that the love of your life has been with you for a couple of hundred years or so. How romantic is that?!

There is a wonderful and very quick thing you can do if you feel you would like to know someone you regard as a soul mate even better. This works with partners and friends, family and even your boss if you think they would be up for it!

📖

- Sit opposite your soul mate.

- Hold their hand and look into their eyes.

- Now soften your eyes and see into the very seat of their soul.

- Does their face change shape?

- Do you have any other impressions of a time or a place?

- Go with what you feel and, when you're ready, break the contact and discuss what you saw with each other.

If the person you think you had a link with isn't around you at the moment, why not try looking into a photograph? Make sure it's large enough to see their face and most importantly their eyes.

This is very powerful, so only do it with those you trust. If you laugh, that's fine – I did the first time I did it! You're laughing because in a way it's uncomfortable, as you would expect when someone looks into your soul and you into theirs, but things will get pretty serious soon enough.

Motivation

OK, it all sounds marvellous so far, so where do you start? Not so fast: there are a few things you need to know before you move on to some practical exercises. And no skipping these pages or you will miss out on some valuable information and karma will bite you on the bum, so there!

You can have a past-life regression just to see what it's like – that's how I started – but then it may be wise to think about what you want from it all before having any more. You might want to think about things like:

- *putting a personal relationship into context*

- *bringing forward and enhancing a skill*

- *explaining phobias and fears (just where did your fear of water come from?)*

- *understanding dreams that may have bothered you for years*

- *verifying historical details*

- *understanding a love for another country.*

The choice is yours, but keeping a sense of structure to your past-life work will make it a very useful tool. Later you will see how I took some of the information I learned and applied it in this life.

Now I can see you nodding off, so why not try this very simple exercise?

- Close your eyes and imagine there's a full-length mirror in front of you, but it's covered with a sheet.

- Let yourself take that image in. Look at the folds of the fabric and the height of the mirror it's covering.

- Now imagine you're staring at that sheet, just staring at it, and as you do so it drops. For a second you catch a glimpse of another face, another shape and different clothes. As quickly as that image appeared, it disappears.

- Remember what you saw. You could meet this character later on.

Roadblocks

I am often asked whether there are people who don't get anything at all from a regression. The answer is no, everyone gets something, although some people say they got nothing and then you have a cup of tea and talk about what happened and they tell you that they saw loads of things but didn't like to say anything at the time! So you can be reassured that you will experience something. Just go with what you see. It may appear random to start with – it often does until the soul decides which part of your cosmic DVD it wants to show you first – but that's just how it works.

Another block can come in the form of the views of those around you. Not everyone is interested in past-life work. Some will think it's total nonsense; some will think it's unnecessary. You should listen to what they have to say and do what you want anyway. Remember you have free will – you have no choice in that!

Also remember that if you're in a past life and you don't want to go any further, it takes just seconds to come out of it – and just minutes to go back in and find out what happened, in my experience.

There are times, however, where you may be too nosey for your own good and in that case your universal spiritual mind will give you an image like a brick wall, a padlocked door or something similar. This is best observed and left alone. You can go round the block and try again when you have learned more about what you're being given.

Respecting this is something I learned the hard way. I had been very busy with my development, but in my haste I had missed out a huge chunk of work – or maybe I couldn't quite grasp it, so perhaps instead of working at it I chose to ignore it. Anyway, what I needed to do was important, but I thought I would leap ten steps ahead anyway, so off I went to do a meditation I was really looking forward to – it was the next stepping stone in my development – and then, as I moved to go through a door into a special place in my meditation, there it was: a padlock. Right across the door. No note saying, 'Be back later,' nothing to say, 'Try round the back,' just a padlock. No matter how hard I tried to move it or just put myself into the room behind it, nothing was happening, so I stopped and, disappointed, called my mentor and teacher, Jenny Shell. She knew instantly why I had been blocked. My wrists were cosmically slapped, I did the work and eventually I moved on – but it was a lesson I've never forgotten!

Chicken and egg

One of the biggest doubts people have about past-life work is the movie theory. You know the one – you've seen *Gladiator* and there you are in your past life fighting a lion or two in ancient Rome and hopefully winning out in the end. The crowds are cheering, the sun is hot, blah, blah, blah. Surely it's just your imagination reminding you of the movie. You've always loved those movies and are saving up to go to the Colosseum, so it's been on your mind, right?

Think about it. What came first, your love of all things Roman or the movie? Chances are, you have always loved a period in time and have been drawn to the movie that matched your own interest.

Personal responsibility

Unlike paying taxes, nobody is going to come along and force you into having a past-life regression. That's entirely your choice, and whether you have one or many more is again your choice. I would advise you to have only one every three months or so, to give yourself time to put into practice what you learn, but it's entirely up to you. You have to make up your own mind on this.

During your regression, find out some facts if you can. Get names and dates, and above all record what you see by writing it down immediately after you finish or, better still, get a mate to write it down as you do the regression, and then return the favour. Be your own investigator or give up at the first hurdle – it's down to that free will again!

Actually, I want to stress the importance of writing things down. It's all too easy at the start of a book to skim-read, but if I repeat it here, there's a chance that you will read at least one of these sentences: *Record your past lives. Write them down! Keep a journal of your past lives.* Write down who you were, where you were, how you think it reflects where you are in your life today and what the lesson could be. This journal will come out when you intuitively need to be reminded of things. Mine does to this very day.

What you learn, of course, is up to your soul. What you do with it is up to your personality and just how motivated you are to make changes in your life. You don't have to tell anyone you're doing past-life regression or you can shout it from the rooftops. You can re-enact your lives at your local amateur dramatic night, if you like. What you do with the information and how you go about it is your choice. Just remember, though, that you're dealing with sacred information about your innermost being and perhaps a certain respect wouldn't go amiss.

So how do you do it?

There are many ways. Hypnosis is probably the best known, but not the one used here. Here it's about creative visualization, creating images that lead your conscious mind to a place where the subconscious and universal minds meet and you can uncover memories of your past.

If you have never done this sort of thing before, don't worry, it's easy enough and the techniques are simple to grasp. With practice they become second nature and you'll find what used to take you 20 minutes comes down to five or so as your subconscious learns to recognize the triggers you have put in place, signs that you're ready to visit your past lives and gain more information for your onward journey.

If you're ready, let's try a little creative visualization...

Make yourself comfortable. Sit up, don't lie down. Put your feet firmly on the floor. Ideally, you should be shoeless. Place your hands palm up either beside you or in your lap and close your eyes.

Take a deep breath in and then hold it for the count of three and let it go, and as you do so, let your shoulders drop, the tension go from your neck and your whole body relax. Then do it again and once more just to make sure.

Now you're fully relaxed, in your mind's eye see your own front door, or the back door if that's the one you use every day.

Look at it in detail, see the fittings and fixtures, note the colour. This door is something you see every day, but I bet you never really take much notice of it — or at least you think you don't.

Keep looking and then imagine touching it. Is it warm? Cold? Are there bits that need your attention?

Spend as long as you like imagining touching your door and when you think you have had enough, simply let the door fade and wiggle your fingers and feet and open your eyes.

Now get up, go to the door and take a look at it in the physical world. Did you see things in your visualization that you hadn't really noticed before?

Touch the door and ponder on the thought that if you can remember something so inanimate in so

*much detail, what can you remember about lives
that have stirred your passions and made you the
person you are today?*

And now, something mundane. Always do something mundane after you have visited your subconscious memory, as it reminds you that you are living in a physical body in a physical world and all the rules associated with that apply. So make a cup of tea and have a biscuit. It works for me and if there's chocolate involved somewhere along the way, then so much the better.

The importance of thought

Visualization shows how powerful our thoughts are. Thoughts generate the world in which we live. Every thought becomes a thing – in other words, when you concentrate hard enough (and sometimes even when you don't), what you think about comes to you. If you are naturally positive, then the way you approach and handle situations will attract positive results. On the other hand, if you expect negative results and behave, look and talk accordingly, that's what the power of your subconscious mind is working towards.

Your past-life regression will bring you images from times long gone, but it's up to you to project the changes you want to make as a consequence into your life right here, right now. So keep a clear idea of what you want in your mind, be sure to reinforce it and don't let negativity in!

Visualizing the changes you want is like dreaming a very realistic dream and making things end up the way you want them to, rather than having a random set of events happen and making the most of them. It puts you in charge rather than lets you be taken for a ride, I suppose. Your imagination is there to be used and the more you use it, the more you get used to using it, and before you know where you are you are back in control in a world that often tries to take that very thing away from us.

Earthbound: there's no point in flying if you don't know how to land

Before you get started with a past-life regression, just a little preparation is required. First you have to know that it's all too easy to get carried away with the process, to be so 'up' with it all that you forget why you started it all in the first place. This isn't something you want – it prevents you from applying what you learn and it stops your growth in the long term – so it's important you learn how to ground yourself before you fly off.

It's also important you have a plan in mind, a reason for taking the trouble to visit your past lives and to know how to bring them into the present. If you fail to be properly prepared, you run the risk of failing to do justice to the information you get.

Coming out of the regression if you feel uncomfortable should be number one on your list of things to remember. If you choose to use a therapist, they will let you know what they need you to do if you want to end the session. Usually it's something as simple as opening your eyes. If you're working on your own or with a friend, come up with your own prompt. For me it's opening my eyes and wiggling my fingers and toes. That reminds me I am in a physical body and of course it stops the pictures forming. I have only had to do this once. It was at a time when I felt emotionally unable to deal with what I was seeing. I didn't feel threatened and never have done, I was just feeling very emotional because of some of the sights I was seeing and needed a break before revisiting that life.

Your belief system is also important to your past-life journey. It's your protection, if you like. Protection is about making you feel more comfortable, giving you a sensation of being looked over and after, which is exactly what is happening when you do past-life work. What are you being protected from, you may ask. I will tell you! Usually you're being protected from wandering away with yourself, that's all. There's nothing nasty waiting in the wings to bite your head off. Protection is really about focusing and controlling your energy and having some sort of intent around your regression so that you can get the most out of it.

Protection is a personal thing. Whether it's angels you use or guides you rely on more heavily or a guiding light you follow makes no difference, as long as you have complete faith in it. That's what's important. If you pay too much attention to someone else's way of doing things it can cause you to be off-balance and to question your own system, and that in turn can knock your confidence. Again, there is only one way and that's *your* way.

Many people don't know how to connect to these beings, even though they recognize that they are around them. To help you to do so, it may be a good idea to try this very simple meditation. Trust what you see, and if you see nothing, do it again when you feel ready. Eventually you will get something.

Make yourself comfortable.

Close your eyes and start to think about your physical body. As you do so, recognize where there is tension. Where do you feel it?

Focus your attention on that area, take a deep breath and send that oxygen to that part of your body. Imagine it as bubbles of light, as a liquid, anything you like, just see it moving to those tense areas and let the tension go, just let it go.

When you feel fully relaxed, imagine you are surrounded by a white light, a powerful all-encompassing white light.

Spend some time in this light, feeling more and more relaxed and comfortable, and when you're ready, imagine a chair, any kind of chair you want, and sit on it.

As you sit in this chair, look ahead of you and now imagine a doorway. It can be any door you like, just put it there in your mind and use the power of your mind to imagine what it would look like.

See an even stronger light coming through the door frame.

Now see the door open. Just let it swing open – and this is where you stop putting in your own images and let them take care of themselves. As the door opens, let whatever forms on the other side of the door form.

You may see an angel, your guide, an animal – it makes no difference – they will appear as they appear. Let them take shape.

Remain seated and wait. If they come towards you, stand up to greet them. They may not move from the doorway, in which case look and remember their form and shape. You can return here any time you want to try to communicate with your guide.

If they do come forward, pay attention to anything they have to say to you and if they ask if you have any questions, go ahead and ask.

When the time is right, your guide will move back through the doorway. Let them go and watch as the door closes behind them.

Now see that door fade away. Let it fade and do the same with your chair.

Immerse yourself once more in that white light. Feel its healing power and surround yourself with the love that it brings.

When you're ready, open your eyes, wiggle your feet, wiggle your fingers and allow yourself a great big smile.

Who was your guide? Have you met them before? What did they have to say to you and how does it fit in with the path you're on at the moment?

Write your experience down and remember that your guide will be with you when you connect to your past lives. You may not see them, but they will be there helping.

Paula

Paula and I worked together. We had a bond and enjoyed each other's company from the start. As time went by we started to talk about past-life work and her interest in all things spiritual came to the fore. She was already using some of her gifts in her job as a beauty therapist and spa manager, as do many therapists. Have you ever wondered why some massages make you feel spaced out? Maybe the therapist is a natural healer or maybe they are using Reiki at the same time as massaging you.

Anyway, back to Paula! She came to me for a regression and, as sometimes happens, she wasn't the only one who got something to think about afterwards...

Paula found herself in Australia. She was an aboriginal man – something she found interesting!

In this life Paula is a slim and very feminine woman who is delicate in her looks, but here she was a mountain of a man who was very muscular. She kept referring to his feet: 'What massive feet!'

Her story unfolded and it became clear she had been the spiritual leader of her tribe, connected strongly to the spiritual realms through her belief system, which included her guides. At the end of her regression she was asked if she wanted to meet her guide from that life, so he came forward – and it was me!

There I was, not looking the same, it has to be said, but I had been her guide in her former life. That gave me something to think about, I can tell you.

Paula and I don't see much of each other these days, but I think of her often and now and again I pick up the phone to see how she is and usually it's a time when she could use someone to talk to.

Your own guides will have a connection to you. It may through a past life, it may be as an interested angelic force or it could be that you have known them in this life; but one thing is for sure – they will have a message for you if you are ready to listen.

Tea, anyone?

I know the tea and biscuits thing that happens after a regression or other spiritual work can sometimes seem as if it has no real purpose other than giving you some sugar after your tiring outing, but don't be misled by this simple technique. Food and drink are important, as they remind us we live on the Earth plane. Do you think your spirit guide goes home for his dinner after a hard day looking over you? With no physical body there is no need for such sustenance, and that's the point – your physical body eats and drinks, and by reminding yourself you are on Earth, you are grounding yourself, or coming in to land.

If ever you feel you're floating off and becoming a bit too wispy or ethereal, you don't have to reach for the biscuits, though. There are other things you can do:

- Add some rock salt to your bathwater.

- Eat good organic food.

- Drink wine.

- Have sex.

- Do some gardening.

- Walk in the wind and rain.

- Go for a swim.

- Stop meditating or doing a lot of spiritual work until you feel more grounded.

There is no point in being so heavenly minded that you are no earthly good.

Going up

There are many levels you can work at with your past lives and hopefully you will see the difference as the examples of my own past lives unfold, but remember that no matter whether it's a full-on regression or a simple meditation for some quick help, they are all equally valid and you should treasure everything you find and of course *write it down!*

The first level is basically what you have just done – a simple meditation to remind yourself of something you have some knowledge of already. No massive preparation is required for this. You don't need anything other than some peace and quiet and the time to invest. OK – that's tough enough to find in today's hectic world!

This level is all about combining your conscious, subconscious and universal mind without giving too much ground to your emotions. It's very useful when you have more than one person regressing at the same time; it makes things easier to control and gives you enough information to show where you may want to visit when it comes to the final level – the full regression.

So, what next?

❯❯❯❯❯❯

CHAPTER 2

THE AKASHIC RECORDS

There is a place you can go where you can gather information and get some glimpses of a life. It's a good place to start because it's like watching a DVD rather than being in a play – it's observing rather than feeling the whole deal. It's where the Akashic records are kept.

I walked along a corridor, dusty and full of strangely familiar objects – a suit of armour over there, a cloak, a staff and in the corner an elaborate headdress, but nothing I could put into any particular place or time – and then I reached a massive door. It opened as if by magic onto a huge circular library and a sylph (an elemental creature that symbolizes air) beckoned me to a desk. I was aware of others moving around this library, but I couldn't really see them, just hear the noise and sense the movement. So I sat down at the appointed desk and there in front of me was a leather-bound book, very large and engraved with many of the objects I had seen in the hallway.

The book opened on its own and on its pages there were no words but moving images – images of different times and situations that were obviously connected to my past lives. That was why I was there, after all. The pages seemed to turn on their own – all I had to do was sit and look in wonder at the images flowing on them.

After minutes, which seemed like hours, I was instructed to leave the book and make my way back to the hallway and ultimately to return my consciousness back into the room where I and several others were experiencing the past-life visualization.

I had seen Atlantis, been to ancient Rome, walked along an English cliff top and sat in the solitary cell of a monk... How enlightening, and I wanted more.

The huge library I had been in holds the soul books of all humanity. Everything you have ever done or said is recorded there and you can visit if and when you choose. Many cultures are aware of such a place, but they may give it another name. That's really unimportant; what *is* important is you know it's there. There is only one to way to know that for sure, of course, and that's to visit it. Makes sense to me! But first let's just revisit one of the lives in my book.

The Akashic record revisited

Here is an account of just one of the lives I saw in my book. Remember, this is a visit to the Akashic records and as such you tend to observe the character rather than see through their eyes as you do when it's a full regression.

Sitting at my book and asking in my mind to see one life, a life my soul wanted me to see, I waited for the images to form...

I was in a market square in Italy, where in Italy I couldn't tell, but it was clearly Italy and even though the square was busy with people I could tell instantly which character was me – he was a priest, a bit of a scruffy one, and to be honest he looked as if he might have needed a bath, which didn't fill me with too much joy, I can tell you! He was obviously not very well, stumbling a little and clearly feverish, but he spoke to everyone who hailed him, ruffled the kids' hair as he passed and accepted some fruit from a kind market trader. Everyone seemed to know him. He made his way to a seat near a fountain and as soon as he sat down he was surrounded by people laughing and joking with him. He had nothing other than the fruit in his hand and the tattered robe on his back, but still he made the effort to get out, to wander around and touch people with his message, which was one of hope, one of belief and one that encouraged those who had even less than him to keep going and to have faith. Faith was the one thing he had in abundance – he was rich beyond his dreams as far as that went – and he was happy to sit there surrounded by people who loved him.

I wanted to stay longer, but time wasn't on my side. The scene changed to one of a graveside where he was being buried. Many people turned out, but the most significant thing to me was what was placed on his grave: a tattered Bible and a pair of sandals. Why? The Bible says, 'Faith,' the sandals say, 'Walk the Earth.'

How did that life reflect my own life at that point? The physical reality of my life was of course far removed from the physical reality of the life of that priest, but emotionally I could understand him. I was working in a job that paid the bills and brought me no joy whatsoever, and what I really wanted was to talk about what I had learned from my training and to share more of that with people, to make a living from it, no matter how modest, and to be master of my own path rather than follow a dictated one.

Shortly afterwards I was lucky enough to be giving a light-hearted talk on astrology at a health resort and to meet Jane Ennis, who was at that point the editor of *Now* magazine, and after just a few weeks I was writing astrology for *Now* readers and suddenly I had options.

Prepare to visit your own soul book

Remember, this is about taking a look at a past life. It's likely to be an opportunity to see one or two lives and establish a starting-point, a place you can move forward from, and it's about your mind, that's all. Your first foray isn't a time to go too deep.

So, make yourself comfortable, sit somewhere you feel happy and content, switch off mobile telephones and unplug the landline if you can – you don't want any distractions.

Close your eyes and breathe in deeply. Hold your breath and let it out, and as you do so, relax your shoulders and let that feeling flow down through your entire body. Feel relaxed.

Now imagine you're in a forest, any forest you like.

Imagine what the trees look like, what smells surround you, what the temperature is, whether there are any animals close by.

Walk along the path that unfolds ahead of you. Follow it until you come to a large tree – it's usually an oak tree, but you can have whatever you want – and notice that it has a door in its base.

Go through the door when it opens for you. It takes you into a room whose black-and-white tile floor is strewn with herbs like rosemary and lavender that release their scent as you walk on them.

Move towards the back of the room where you will see an altar covered with a simple white cloth. Burning in the centre of it is a single blue flame.

Pause here and ponder the journey you're about to take. Then look up and see three doors in front of you, behind the altar. Walk towards the one on the left.

As you approach, it opens and on the other side you see an orange globe, a sphere of swirling light. Step inside it.

As you do so, it begins to rise up. Don't worry, you're perfectly safe, just enjoy the peace and calm that surround you as you move through the ether.

Gently you feel the sphere land and almost as soon as you do it melts away to reveal a frozen land-scape, a desert of ice and snow in which there appears to be another path ahead of you. This time it's strewn with words, phrases, poetry and musical notes. Follow the path.

Ahead of you there's an almighty rumble and in the near distance you see a giant library rise up from the ice. It's circular and surrounded by stairs leading up to pillars that have doors behind them — lots of stairs, pillars and doors.

Move towards the doorway you are drawn to. Walk carefully, but be sure of your intention. If you see other images, take note and go with them if it feels right, but try to come back to the path when you're aware of it again.

Move up to the door and take note of what it's like. Are there any engravings on it? The door will open and you will find yourself in a hallway.

Either side of this hallway there are artefacts from your past lives. Have a look and try to remember some of them, as they too will offer you some clues.

Move towards yet another door at the back of the hallway and wait until your Akashic guide comes to greet you.

Follow them to your book, thank them for their attendance and turn your attention to the desk in front of you.

Look at your book. Is there a name on it? Touch it. How does it feel?

The book will open and reveal whatever it has to reveal to you. Allow about five minutes of silence to spend with your record. That may not seem long, but it will be ample and once you learn the route you can come back whenever you feel the need.

When you are ready to leave, allow your book to close and follow your Akashic guide out of the library. At the door thank them for their help and walk down your hallway once more, taking note of anything you might have missed on the way in.

*Leave the Akashic library and go down the steps
and back into your orange sphere. Let it surround
you and take you back into the room at the bottom
of your tree.*

*Walk out of the room and back into your forest.
Follow the path and as you move along it, let it
melt away and slowly bring your consciousness back
into the here and now.*

How was that for you?

Write down what you saw, and when you have, make that tea and eat a biscuit. In fact have another one for me!

As you do so, think of the following:

- *What did you learn that could explain how you feel in this life?*

- *Does it explain a talent or a love for a place in history or an area?*

- *What about fears and phobias – did the root cause show itself?*

- *Have you had dreams about these places or people?*

Whenever things come to you, make sure you keep a record of them. All the details will tie up eventually and your life theme will become glaringly obvious.

An Egyptian account

When Vanessa first came to me she was interested in past lives simply because I had told her of my experiences. Although she did want to know more, she wasn't sure quite how it would help her in this life.

She found herself in ancient Egypt and even though she had a position of some authority in a temple it was in title only; truth is, she was nothing more than a decoration to some and a nuisance to others. Of course, she felt differently – she longed to do what she wanted rather than what was expected of her. She tried to rebel once or twice, but she was always severely punished and brought back into line, so pretty soon she did as she was told and that was that.

Her role as a figurehead in temple rituals was fascinating to observe. She fulfilled it perfectly and even enjoyed her worship. The intricate moves and gestures were fascinating for her to watch.

Eventually a love story began, the man involved being someone whom she perhaps shouldn't have got involved with, but there you go – it happens! He was not only of low birth, he was also close to her father, working for him on a daily basis. She decided to break free of her gilded cage, running away with the love of her life, which wasn't an easy thing to do.

Did she succeed or did it all go wrong? Intrigue and passion as it all turned sour would have made a good story, but a better one was the truth: yes, she did succeed and ended her days with children and a husband who adored her, but more importantly she had her freedom and that was what she remembered most of all from that life.

So how did it help her? Vanessa found her regression particularly interesting because at the time she was feeling hemmed in by different circumstances and felt she had no real options. After the regression she realized there is always an option and decided that rather than do what everyone else wanted her to do, she was going to say 'no'. It may not seem like much, but up to that point she had been playing the dutiful princess, doing as she was told and going through the rituals she had been conditioned to go along with. Although there was no man involved in her decision, he turned up eventually. That's all I'm saying!

Unmasking the bully

There is no doubt that part of what you learn from your past life will be interesting and great coffee-table chat. That's easy to deal with, but what about when a past life throws up some challenging options for you now? Like Vanessa, you may have to turn a lifetime of conditioning on its head, years spent saying 'yes' when in fact you wanted to say 'no'.

Sometimes past-life influences can act like a bully; they suggest that any wavering from the way things are normally done will result in danger. They do it from deep within your subconscious, shaking their metaphorical fist every time you even think of moving out of your comfort zone. They will keep you doing the same thing over and over again until you name and shame them. Vanessa stopped and recognized the bully, and that's what you have to do too.

Like all bullies, the thing to do is to turn and confront them, to show them you're not scared of them. One little action of bravery could very soon snowball into full-blown confidence and result in you taking action where previously you gave up, most of the time not even knowing why.

To help you, try this little meditation. It should give you the courage you need when you have to go against your outworn habits and patterns.

Sit comfortably, breathe in and hold your breath and then release it. Do this again and drop your shoulders. Take the tension out of your body. Just relax.

See yourself in your lovely forest. Be there. Imagine the light coming through the trees, all the sounds and sights... Is it warm or cold?

Walk along the path and with every step relax a little more. Be present in the moment and enjoy the peace and calm of this special place.

In the distance you can see what looks like a house. It's rickety, uncared-for and seems out of place in your forest. Walk towards it and investigate.

Now you're at the house you see the roof needs some attention and the windows don't look that clean, but you're determined to go inside, so in you go!

Have a good look around the rooms. Is there anything in them? Maybe there are things you recognize as being yours, perhaps things you somehow feel you lost a long time ago?

Now become aware of a door, a door underneath the stairs, probably leading to a cellar or basement. Move towards it and open it.

Go down the staircase – have no fear, it's light, you can see perfectly well – and keep going down and down until you reach the bottom, and there in the corner is your bully.

What do they look like? What are they doing? They are probably trying to hide because they know why you are here. You are here to mark the end of their rule, a cessation of all their tricks and their domination of the fears that have held you back for too long.

Hold out your hand, let them come to you, and as they do, smile – yes, smile. Now thank them for being the custodian of your reluctance, the holder of your helplessness and for getting you to where you are today.

Then let them know they are no longer the one making those decisions. Surround your bully in a bubble of light. Make it a pink light, see them smile back and watch them transform, their job done. Accept any apology they may give you – and it should be an apology, by the way; excuses are not accepted!

Your bully will disappear. Let them and make your way back up the stairs and into the house.

As you emerge from the basement you will see the rooms changed. Now they are beautifully decorated, comfortable and in good order.

Walk from the house and as you wander through the garden look back at it. It's now fully restored and you're happy to have it in your forest, a place of sanctuary.

Walk away from the house now, back down your path into the forest, and as you walk, feel lighter, feel free, feel ready to make your own choices without fear of those who may seek to stop you. Let the forest fade away and bring your consciousness back into the here and now.

Kettle on, biscuits out. How do you feel? Consolidate your experiences by writing them down. Pay particular attention to your feelings. Are they physical? Do you actually feel lighter, as if a burden has been lifted?

Remember, this isn't about regret, it's about understanding. Realize that your bully was always part of you and therefore it could only be you who set it free and took back the power as well as the responsibility for all your actions. As you move forward, the more you realize that, the quicker you will proceed.

))))))

CHAPTER 3

ONE STEP AT A TIME

Each person experiences the regression process in their own way. Some see more, others hear more, and so on. We all have our memories served up a different way and that can dictate how deeply we live our regressions. Some people feel exhausted afterwards, some feel elated. Me, I'm worn out and know not to schedule anything else in for at least a couple of hours afterwards. But remember that no matter what you get or what you think you don't get, any regression is a good one.

When you're learning to drive, the first thing you have to do is learn how to brake, and it's the same for past-life regression – the full-on emotional one, that is. It's not likely that you're heading for a crash, so there's no need to panic, it's more about learning to deal with things that you may not feel too comfortable with but you know the learning you are getting is worth the intensity that can sometimes be experienced within a PLR (Past-Life Regression – let's use that abbreviation from now on).

Frequently asked questions

CAN I GET STUCK?

No, you can't get stuck. You will always come back to your normal existence. It's like losing yourself in a really good movie, then coming into the bright lights of the foyer – you still remember how it all went and how it made you feel, but you soon start to focus on reality and where you parked the car, as well as will the chip shop still be open because you're starving!

WHAT IF I AM RECEIVING THERAPY OR TAKING ANTI-DEPRESSION MEDICATION?

You must discuss the benefits you expect to get from your PLR before you have one with the professional who's treating you and go with their advice.

WILL I BE UNCONSCIOUS?

No, you won't. You'll know you are having a regression, but at the same time you'll be able to hear what's going on in the room or outside in the street. If you do nod off, that's about your energy levels, so make sure you do your PLR when you feel up to it. If you've been overworking it's not a good idea to have one, as you will fall asleep!

WHAT IF I DON'T LIKE WHAT I SEE?

Well, take a look at this... Here's an awkward life of mine:

My sister and I were playing by the river, enjoying the sunshine and splashing away as our mother washed some clothes nearby. Then out of nowhere came three men on horseback. One of them grabbed at me as I ran away from him but missed, so he got off his horse and chased me. I was fast, but no match for his strength and power, and he caught me. He had his arms around mine to stop me from punching him, so I kicked him instead, but he hit me back and I slumped broken, accepting my fate.

I don't know what happened to my sister or my mother, I never saw them again and aged 12 I was chained and made to walk and walk and walk... Eventually I found myself in a market square with people poking and prodding at me, checking my teeth and giving me the most intimate examinations, which I obviously objected to. 'Spirit' they called it; 'self-respect' was my view on the subject.

An older man approached. He was looking for a houseboy, someone to do the lowliest of tasks whilst looking immaculate enough to stand beside him to impress his friends when they called for tea, which they did daily. So that's what I became.

I got through it by blocking out any emotion, for even hatred was useless. I just felt nothing, nothing at all. I simply got up in the morning, did what I had to do and went to bed at night. That was my life. Until I had a bright idea, a solution to my dilemma that was brought about in the blink of an eye: I cut my master's throat.

That was that. I left.

Maybe I could have sneaked out in the night, perhaps I could have bound him where he could have been found and set free the next day, but no, I killed him.

I was shocked at this during the regression, appalled at my actions. I felt quite sick, but I had to go on to find out what happened to this young man for whom until this point I had felt real sympathy.

Into the night I ran and ran, with blood on my hands from the knife. I ran until I could run no more and then it hit me, the whole event, the full force of all the emotions I had been feeling – or perhaps not feeling would be a better way of putting it – and then that moment, again and again that moment, the knife lying there by his bread waiting to cut nothing more than his supper being used to cut his throat...

I wept and wept and cried myself to sleep, but I was free.

The next day I could hear the dogs barking and getting very excited as they drew closer to me and I knew they would catch up with me and they did. I was shot on sight and that was that.

I could see myself lying on the ground and I watched as white light surrounded me and I moved towards it, but I didn't want to go. I had killed a man and the consequences were surely to go to hell? In the light I could see him, the man I had killed, beckoning me forward, but I thought it was a trap. I could see him, but I was sure all he wanted was to harm me. But then, thinking about it, what more could he do?

So I followed and he embraced me, telling me he understood and he apologized for his behaviour – his behaviour! OK, I had killed him, he said, but it was out of frustration and in the face of tyranny.

I could not accept his reasoning and threw myself on his mercy. He just repeated what he had said earlier and left.

I was left in the light and there I saw my mother and sister. They had died in the attack on the village, trampled by horses and drowned in the very river that had brought us life for so long. I cried and cried and cried, both in the regression and in my current life, until I screamed – a scream with hundreds of years of anguish behind it.

There could be some difficult things to confront in your past lives, make no mistake; but remember, you're the one who is control of the situation and if you feel in any way uncomfortable you can break your visualization at any time. If this happens you'll be fine and I'm sure you will find that even though it was tough, you will want to know more. If you feel more comfortable with the Akashic Records visualization, maybe you could use that one to get more information. That may be easier, as it's more about the head than the heart.

Sometimes you do need to go back into a difficult past life, ask the questions, look at the lessons you learned and decide how to apply the positive ones in this life. 'What could be a positive lesson from that houseboy's life?' I hear you ask. I learned that I had a threshold and whilst I was sure things weren't going to be so dramatic in this life, I realized that taking action early was better for me than letting things build to an explosive level.

In my life at that time I had been feeling odd. The pain of separation was with me and yet nobody in my life had died or was leaving for any reason, so I put the purpose of this regression down to making me feel lighter, removing the karmic pressure, if you like, and that was that.

Sometime later the echoes from that life did catch up with me when I was bullied and put upon for something I didn't do, and had nowhere to go, or at least I thought I hadn't.

There's nothing big or clever about picking on someone else simply because you can, because you think the authority of your position or some other trumped-up reason means you are better than anyone else. My dad always taught me I was no better or worse than anyone else, but it takes some doing to remember that all of the time.

Back then my boss was making things difficult to say the least, working me into the ground and doing less and less himself. He made my life hell and I put up with it until I began to realize my creativity was being stifled as well as my energy and my ability to simply be myself. I had become moody, difficult with my mates when I actually did see them and, worst of all, short-tempered with my partner. I recognized that something had to give and, remembering the lessons from my past life, I took a break, a few days off to spend in silent contemplation and to visit my family.

I sat on a beautiful hillside in my native Scotland, watched the sheep and looked at the river running through the valley. I had instinctively gone to a place I had visited as a child, a place that had happy memories. I sat there and contemplated life – what was important and just what I was doing, and even though I had nothing to move on to, I trusted in the fact that I was in the wrong place and needed to do something about it. Rather than carry on festering until I walked out or got angry and made a fool of myself, I admitted it wasn't right for me – and I made a plan.

I went to a little post office, bought a pen, paper and an envelope, wrote out my resignation and sent it there and then.

I worked freelance until something new came along, and it did, but more importantly, I was human again and back in control.

What happened to my old boss? Karma. It's easy to think I hated him and wanted him to suffer, but the truth is I didn't care. I was truly at peace with my decision and happy to move away from the situation. It's a shame I hadn't thought or done the same all those hundreds of years ago.

So this difficult life in the past actually brought me a practical way of dealing with life in the present. To deal with unexpected events I now have a three-step plan:

Look.

Listen.

Leap.

1. Look at what is truly going on. Take a step back and think about the situation and what you could gain from it, if anything. Look at the characters involved and think about what you can say or do to convince them to change their mind or perhaps to do what you're doing. Wait a while, run different scenarios through your head and of course trust in your intuition.

2. Listen to your intuition. Even if it's bringing you some tough choices, trust that it knows best. Then listen to those you can confide in. Run your course of action by them. Good friends will tell you how they see it without fear, and that is something to cherish.

3. Leap into action as soon as you have your plan, as soon as you have your plan, as soon as you have your plan – that's no typing error, it had to be said three times for you to get it! Procrastination is where things usually go wrong. If you give more negative thoughts time to fester they will inevitably bring you doubt, and doubt brings inaction, and that means you

are whipped up by the tide of events rather than riding the waves towards a destination of your own choosing.

HOW DO I RELEASE FEARS AND NEGATIVITY DURING A PLR?

That is part of your regression. At the end you will be asked to do just that.

WILL I BE A DIFFERENT SEX?

There's a fifty-fifty chance on that one! You can be either sex, young, old, tall, short, whatever. Chances are that unless you ask to go back to a life you have already experienced, you will get a different one each time, and even when you do ask for the same one, sometimes you don't get it!

WILL I DEFINITELY HAVE HAD A PAST LIFE?

If you have picked up this book and are thinking about having one, you will have had one – in fact you're likely to have had hundreds. A very young soul, with few incarnations or lessons learned, wouldn't be interested in past-life work.

WILL I SEE ANYONE I RECOGNIZE FROM THIS LIFE?

You may very well recognize someone. Make a note if you do, as this will of course be very important; but remember, they were a different personality in that life even though you will recognize some character traits from their current one!

Afterwards

OK, that's enough questions for now. You need to know now what to do when you finish your regression. There is no doubt you will be excited and you will probably have more questions than answers, but there are some things you need to do.

First things first: write down what happened. Make it as brief or as in-depth as you feel you can. Do this with the obligatory cup of tea and a biscuit – remember, the simple act of eating and drinking reminds your conscious mind it's back in the here and now. You can add more when you remember it, so keep your notebook handy and when you do remember things, for goodness's sake, write them down immediately!

If you are one of those people who gets tired after a PLR, allow yourself the time to rest. Maybe even drift off into sleep for half an hour or so. Sometimes this brings even more information for me, which I write down immediately, of course!

Be sure of yourself when you get your information. You may think you've imagined the lot – and there is really no way of knowing other than confirming the information – but even if you did imagine it, surely the symbolism and imagery come from somewhere and your inner being is trying to tell you something.

If you think it's all your imagination, that's fine as long as you do something with what you are given – and that's the true key to all inner work. Listen to that still voice that urges you to make some changes, and when it feels right, follow it.

With or without a therapist?

There are two ways of having your regression – no right or wrong, just two ways of doing it. My first one was with a therapist, someone in the room actually going through the regression with me, asking questions and helping me along. I would recommend this for your first regression, as it will give you confidence and help you figure out what you yourself should be looking for.

Choose your therapist wisely. Go with someone who comes with a recommendation if you can. If you don't know anyone who has had a PLR and can recommend someone, ask at your local esoteric bookstore. They will know some great people, I'm sure.

The second method is of course to go it alone. I will give you some excellent meditations to follow in this book and even though the first few times can sometimes be slow, you will soon pick up the technique and find it an easy way to access your past lives and all the information they hold. If you want, you can do this with a friend. Choose someone you trust. They will be hearing some amazing things about you and you don't want that to be the hot topic of office gossip next day.

To give you an idea, here is an account of my very first regression, which was actually performed by a lady called Anne in Portsmouth many years ago.

When I arrived I realized that Anne had prepared the room ready for me. Incense burned and candles glowed, and as she welcomed me into her home I felt relaxed already. In the background, beautiful music was playing and although I was a little apprehensive, I was ready.

Anne began with an exercise in meditation to help me relax and to open up my energy ready for the regression. (This will form part of your practice too.)

After another short meditation she asked me to tell her when I felt ready to begin. Here's how it went:

AG: What are you wearing on your feet?

DW: Sandals, rough and worn.

AG: Are you inside or out?

DW: Outside. It's warm and there's a noise in the distance.

AG: What is the landscape like?

DW: It's dry. There's some grass and some dusty ground. It's hilly. I can't see the sea.

AG: What about the noise you mentioned, what is it?

DW: Sounds like people screaming. Horses' hooves. Think it's a battle

AG: Are you alone?

DW: No, I have my horse with me.

AG: Are there any other human beings with you?

DW: No, but I am on my way to see someone. A woman, I think.

AG: Move forward to that point and tell me where you find yourself.

DW: I'm in a room. It's very well decorated and lit by oil lamps that are giving off a smell. There's a woman in the room. She is very beautiful and she is smiling at me.

AG: Do you recognize this woman?

DW: She is my lover. I think she is an ex of mine from this life.

AG: You mean you recognize her from your current life?

DW: Yes.

AG: Just remember that and now tell me what is happening next.

DW: She is kissing me and asking me if I want to bathe. I am very, very dirty and say yes. She helps me undress and washes my wounds. I know I have been in a battle, one which I just know we won.

AG: Who is 'we'?

DW: I am Greek. I was fighting with the Greek army.

AG: Carry on.

DW: I ache a little and I am exhausted and want to sleep. She beckons me to her bed and I lie down. She kisses me tenderly and leaves me. I fall asleep instantly.

AG: Move on to the following morning.

DW: I am getting dressed in new clothes. I am wearing a fresh white wrap-around skirt thing with a tunic over the top. I feel rested and ready to go.

AG: Go where?

DW: Home to my wife.

AG: So this woman isn't your wife?

DW: Erm, no, she isn't.

AG: OK, go to your wife then.

DW: I can see her. She looks worried, but brightens when she sees me. She smiles as I wrap my arms around her and hug her. There are children there too – five of them.

AG: Do you recognize your wife or any of the children?

DW: I think one of the children is a friend of mine and one is most definitely my mum! How bizarre. (I cry at this point.)

AG: Why are you crying?

DW: The children, they are so sweet and I am such a monster.

AG: Why are you a monster?

DW: I am cheating on their mother and I don't know why.

AG: Take a deep breath and carry on when you're ready.

DW: I am in a room with some other soldiers now. There are two generals I recognize as friends of mine in this life. They aren't very happy about my relationship with the woman. They say she is dangerous and must be stopped, her influence over the king is too great.

AG: Which king is it?

DW: I can see him, but can't see his face.

AG: What is the year?

DW: It feels about a thousand years before Christ. Can that be right?

AG: Go with what you feel. Now what's happening?

DW: These generals are saying she must die. I storm off to warn her.

AG: Go on.

DW: I am in her room. She is listening to me and smiling. She has heard it all before and beckons me to join her on a sort of daybed thing. She offers me some wine that has been left for her and I take a sip. (Here I pause and become distressed.)

AG: What's wrong?

DW: My stomach is sore, my throat is burning. I think I have been poisoned.

AG: You don't have to physically feel the pain. Just see the memory and tell me what's happening.

DW: I have drunk what was meant for her. She didn't do it intentionally, I think it was an accident. I die.

AG: Watch yourself die and tell me what you see.

DW: I am lying on the floor. She is upset and runs for her guards. They come and take me away to another room.

AG: Can you see a light?

DW: Yes, it's in the corner of the room I am now in. It's coming towards me.

AG: Let it completely surround you, let it be all you see, and tell me when you have done that.

DW: OK.

And that is where I am going to leave it. What happens next comes later in the book and opens up another range of fantastic gifts you can expect from a past-life regression.

Looking back on that life, I was struck by several things. Today infidelity isn't something that would ever enter my head. I am and always will be the faithful sort, but I have been the victim of infidelity in two of my major relationships – is this karma or carelessness? Either way, I could have continued in that vein, but decided I no longer wanted to deal with it. I have probably had that karmic hangover for many centuries and it's time to say bye-bye. I cut the strings that bound that one to me and I am pleased to say I now have someone in my life whom I trust implicitly. (How you cut those ties will be discussed later. It's a very useful technique and sends a definite message to your subconscious!)

My current relationship with two of the people who were my children in that life is very strong and I am hugely protective of both these people now and they are very supportive of me.

Spiritually, that life taught me that falling foul of selfishness isn't to be encouraged. Then I was single-minded to the point where others' feelings meant little. I could see them but didn't care too much. I was driven by my own needs and desires rather than those of the people around me.

We aren't made to stand alone, all of us need some human interaction, but the key is the ebb and flow, not the constant outpouring of one to the detriment of another. It's good to be unselfish, but it doesn't mean you have to think of others to the point where your own needs are ignored either – it's about balance.

I have learned through that life to bend rather than remain fixed, and it is still tough sometimes, but I smile when I catch myself being 'a little too Greek' as I now call it. Habits, no matter how many centuries old, can be broken.

CHAPTER 4

CHALLENGING LIVES

What happens when you get information that gives you more food for thought than even the most gluttonous neophyte can cope with? What happens when a life poses you real challenges?

There is no doubt that some lives stick in your head more than others. They are meant to, as the challenges they present you with will bring you more learning in your current life. Sometimes these lives are called your 'key lives'. Clearly they have more of an impact on your current life than most; they also have the potential for your greatest leaps forward.

Matthew was wondering whether there was anything in past lives or not, so he came along for a regression. He went very, very far back, so far back he was wearing animal skins and his language was very limited – he was a cave woman! After recovering from the shock of being female, he started to tell his tale...

Ostracised from his tribe, he was a loner. His – or maybe I should say 'her' – only crime was being different from the rest: her colouring was lighter and she was much taller than most. Learning to live on her own, she began to put more and more distance physically between her and everyone else, and eventually she was out there by herself.

One day she was found by a new group and, being a loner, attracted some interest, particularly from the males in the group, who took their pleasure where they found it. These people soon moved on, leaving her broken and pregnant, and when the baby came she was no longer alone but still lonely, bitter but determined to keep going despite being an outcast. She raised her son to be a fine strong boy and died knowing he would survive.

After the regression Matthew acknowledged the lessons he learned from that life and is now using in his current life: he is independent and enjoys his own company but now balances it out with many friends and a very close family – his new tribe. He is extremely tolerant of those who are different in any way and will go out of his way to help them when he can.

This was a challenging regression and the woman's solitude wasn't comfortable to watch, but Matthew rose to the opportunity this knowledge presented and I always smile when once again he has about an hour to spend with me before he is off to see someone else.

Once you understand the concept of karma you will begin to see things differently, to look at your daily life and see your relationships with those around you in a new light. Don't limit yourself to the here and now of your current incarnation; by looking back at some of the people you have known and the situations you have found yourself in in the past, you will learn more about your own habits and cycles and decide whether or not you want to break them or encourage them to grow!

Bringing forward

What about skills and talents in past lives? Can you use them in the present? What if you were French in a former life – could you go back to that life, remember how to speak French and bring it back? Wouldn't that be great?

Unfortunately, you can't do that. It just doesn't work that way. What a past-life regression can do, though, is show you what you may have a gift for, and if it's languages, then maybe learning one you spoke in a former life would come naturally to you.

For years, for example, I ignored the Tarot and even though the cards formed part of my training I never really took to them. Then I had a regression to a life where I used them a lot and always at the command of another – it's what I was kept around for. I passed on the information to order until one fateful day when yet again I was summoned to do the Tarot and say what I saw. Unfortunately for me, what I saw wasn't what my lord and master wanted me to see, and that was that – off I went to exile and eventual death. You can understand why I didn't want to use the cards from then on!

Then one day in this life I was given a deck by a friend. I picked them up and they felt like old friends, and when I realized they were a tool for understanding my own subconscious rather than for predicting the tall dark handsome stranger stuff we often associate with them, I grew to love them. The regression had unlocked my ability, but it was training and practice that made it real.

Remembering a road less travelled

There are some lives that could surprise or perhaps shock you, some that may have content you find hard to digest, tough to take or so intense you can't shake it for days. Are these sent just to get those reactions or to help you shake your doubts?

For the serious seeker, there always seems to be one life that brings faith where there was lack of conviction, trust where there was hesitancy and clarity where there was confusion. You won't know when you'll find it, where you're likely to be in it or how many regressions you are likely to have first, but you will know it when you experience it!

Here's the tale I started right at the beginning of the book – and this time I am going to tell you it in story form, which is how I remember it best:

Being handed over to the woodsman seems all too real to me still. I can recall the confusion and the hurried bundling of a small baby in rough sacking, then the sneaking out under the cover of darkness, the trees seeming to whisper in the breeze, gossiping and spreading the news amongst themselves. It was the year 500 and I was in England...

Arriving at a warm and comfortable cottage, I could see myself being handed to the woodsman's wife, an ample woman who smelled of flour and love. She took to me immediately and I to her.

Fast forward 12 years to one of those nights where the full moon hangs heavy in the skies and the forest is alive with noise, not knowing if it's day or night, and there I was asleep in my bed, which seemed to shrink as every day I grew taller! From outside the door I heard my name being called, and then again, so I followed it into the silver night.

Coming to a clearing, I met an old and wise man, a man who merely smiled and brought out a necklace, a Celtic pendant engraved with a chalice and a cross, which he pressed into my hand. I asked him what it was, but he just put his fingers to his lips to silence me and bade me sit down on a tree trunk nearby. Here he introduced himself and told me I was to come to him at this spot every night and learn. Learn what? Suffice to say, some of the gifts he imbued me with I still use today.

At 15, I was deemed ready to go into the big wide world, to visit the places my woods-man and his wife had held me back from, to see the world outside the forest that had been my home for many years. So off I went, the old man by my side.

We eventually arrived at a city wall. The city itself looked more like a fortress and the stench coming from it made my stomach churn and my head swim, but on we pressed until we came to a rather fine-look-ing house. This, I was told, was my mother's home.

I was pressed inside and even though I knew what was coming I was still scared and more than a little emotional. Suddenly there she was. She was even more beautiful than I had heard, her red hair plaited on her head and her skin as pale as milk. She looked at me, her eyes full of tears, and came towards me, hugging me until I could barely breathe, a hug I didn't return.

Stepping back, she acknowledged my anger and my bewilderment at why I had been deserted, and sat down, beckoning me to join her. Taking my hand, she began to explain. I am not going to discuss this, as it was intensely personal, but I began to soften, to take her at her word, and besides, by now I was trained to know when someone was being less than honest and I knew she was telling me the truth.

No sooner had I talked to her, though, than I was whisked away, back onto my horse and into the night, but with the promise of a return visit whenever I chose, and this time she would come to me.

I was taken to a building set on a hill, another grand place, and as I approached the door was opened and there waiting to meet me was a monk, an ordinary monk with nothing fancy, nothing noteworthy about him at all. He took me to a cell. I was to be admitted to a monastery to complete my training. But this was no ordinary monastic order, despite appearances to the contrary.

Over the next few years I followed their ways, learning not only devotional study but also the practical use of occult knowledge, which seemed odd to me as nobody ever left this place! Except me. Aged 21, I was deemed ready to go, to get out and walk my path and to see what the universe had in store for me.

These were harsh times. As well as my occult studies I had been trained in swordsmanship, but to be honest I wasn't very good at it – I wasn't built for it!

And so I embarked on my journey. At this point my regression speeded up and I was shown snippets of me talking to people, having a moment of fear when I was attacked and robbed, losing everything, finding love, losing love, etc., etc. Life, really!

Then I came to a moment in time when I was standing in front of a council of men, all dressed as I was, all trained as I was and all looking at me rather than me looking at them, if you know what I mean. Was I worthy, did I have enough knowledge and enough devotion, or at least enough to make what wasn't working work? By this time I was a strong man, able and confident in my abilities but aware of my limits as well as the strengths of those around me.

Nevertheless, I was elected to lead their order – and before all you Da Vinci Code lovers get onto it (don't get me started on that), no, it wasn't the Knights Templar! It was a simple order of warrior monks with purpose and pathways to a higher cause using esoteric principles and laws.

There is much more to this story, so much more, but that's for another book at another time. Here is the point of the life as I see it.

For me, this life was a key one. The difference between a key life and one that simply shows you the truth of what you are getting is hard to put into words. It's more of a feeling, a sense of a certain life being right for you. A key life shows you the challenges or gifts for living this life. It's clear to me, for example, that the teachings in that life paralleled some of those I have in my current incarnation. It's also clear that then as now I travelled and talked about my belief systems and used the knowledge I had acquired in practical ways on a daily basis.

Key lives also show you yourself. Knowing yourself is one the greatest gifts past-life work will bring you and it is the cornerstone of all spiritual growth. So take what you learn and move forward – knowing yourself isn't an excuse to be lazy! 'I always do that' and 'That's just like me' are excuses. Your past lives will always find you out – you'll be able to see your less favourable habits and exactly when you indulged in them. But now you can do something about them!

Pride can often get in the way here. Some people fail to back down when it would be the right thing to do, to give in or to go back to restore the balance between who they are now and who they were in the past. But making your peace, both with yourself and with others, could rely on accepting your failures and offering the cup of change. And if you could turn your deficiencies into blessings, just imagine what you could achieve in the future!

In this search for knowledge and wholeness, you will find there will be one particular life that brings you back into balance and shows you where your true devotion lies. Sooner or later everyone finds it. When you call upon it, you realize anything is possible and nothing really matters. That's your central life, the one everything spins around.

The central life

Your central life brings you into a state of equilibrium, a place where you can deal with anything the universe throws at you, maybe not with ease but certainly with wisdom.

Here's an example. Some time ago I was working with some people whom I respected and thought were in some way better than me at what they did, and I looked to them for inspiration and learning. Turned out they had other agendas and turning back to help someone wasn't one of them, and so I spun out of control, swinging from one side to the other and back again in terms of my own character. I wasn't sure what to do for the best. Did I want to please them or please myself? In the end I remembered this monastic life – remembered not only my knowledge but also who I was – and I chose to please myself.

Self-realization is liberating. When you find that point, when you really know yourself, anything is possible, and dealing with disappointment, temptation, criticism, you name it, becomes so much easier.

Being devoted to the work I did and how I did it, maintaining my point of balance and remaining aware of who I was – this was the lesson of my central life and it was a lesson I would have to learn and be tested on for many lives to come! Even today I am knocked off-balance by other people's stuff, but I find my way back to myself when the bells ring loudly enough for me to notice what's going on.

To give another example, this is the past life of a young woman called Wendy:

Looking up was uncomfortable. It wasn't the blood, wasn't the obvious pain, it was the eyes. Looking into them, she could see the wrong, see the hurt and see the betrayal of one human by another. As a Roman soldier she was used to seeing such things, but this time she had been close to the man now crucified and dying in front of her. She had listened to him talk and had been moved by his words.

Her mind was full of questions and her heart was breaking as she described the moments leading to this horrible event and its ultimate end. These questions would be hard for her to resolve and to equate with her own life, and no matter who was on the cross it was another person being tortured for their beliefs – tortured over a difference of opinion and nothing more.

It was a shock to be seeing such horror, especially as this was a quiet and very peaceful young woman with strong pagan beliefs, a woman who was expecting a Wiccan or perhaps a pagan life that would reflect where she was in her life right now, and the associations with Jesus of Nazareth were too close for comfort. Initially, she went into denial, failing to see the truth or the lesson, but after a couple more regressions and some counselling she began to understand the reasons behind what she had seen.

Wendy's beliefs were everything to her. She accepted other religions and faiths but thought they were off-track and that was that. But now she realized her faith was just her faith for this incarnation and in other lives she would have had, and will have, lots of ways back to her god, or indeed goddess, and that was just fine. Her balancing point was recognizing the beauty in diversity whilst being devoted to her own way – perfect balance.

In her current life this brought her enormous peace. There was no more struggling to prove herself and self-realization once more won the day. Her central life was showing her that others' sacrifices for their beliefs were as valid as hers were for Wicca.

Whoever we are and have been, bringing our feelings and thoughts into balance is going to help things move forward evenly. Think of an aircraft landing. If the left wing is thoughts and the right is feelings, how would you land if one was favoured over the other? The central point of balance is what you're looking for, and that's what your central life can give you.

☽ ☽ ☽ ☽ ☽ ☽

CHAPTER 5

COURAGEOUS LIVES

We all have moments in our life where we have to stand up to tyranny, to those who think they have a right to tell us what to do, even if that goes against every fibre of our being. Do these lives teach us to be strong or do they show our weaknesses? Or are they simply a product of their time? They do usually come from a time when humanity was still warring and fighting on a daily basis – not that we're any further advanced now, but that's another book.

Here is an example, one of my lives where strength won out over adversity:

I was taken to the dressing room, in my mid-teens and small, very small – one of the first things I noticed was my height, barely 5' 6", which is almost a foot shorter than I am now. I was of very slight build, hardly a warrior's build, but there I was putting on my armour and holding my head high and trying not to let anyone see I was scared – very scared.

I was handed a sceptre and my cloak was adjusted behind me, then there was a fanfare and the doors ahead of me were thrown open. There was the court waiting for me to enter the great hall and claim the throne that was mine by birthright. It was a small kingdom in England in the sixth century.

I walked down the line of courtiers, a ragtag bunch if ever there was one, and every so often I could see red eyes looking back at me, which I took to mean those people meant me harm, beware.

I approached the throne and took my seat ready to be crowned by a warlord who looked like a mountain next to me but I knew him to be a good and kind man and had no fear. He raised the crown and placed it on my head. It slipped across my eyes and I had to push it back onto my head. Then I rose and the court dropped to its knees in front of its new king.

I had no sense of power or ego. I didn't feel better than the people in front of me at all. In fact what I actually felt was the desire to run away, to take to the hills and never come back, but this was my destiny and I had been told it many times by some of those watching me. But was it my destiny, I wondered, or their own agenda?

My father was dead, my mother was only just starting to know me again – something that has occurred with some regularity in my lives, particularly with lives of any power – and as for friends, I had nobody in the world I could trust, which made me feel lonely most of the time. But I was unable to cry; crying wasn't allowed. Solitude brings the gift of concentration, but at what price?

And so I moved into the knights' hall to meet my champions, all vying for position and all promising allegiance to the crown. But what about the head under the crown?

Of course I had my advisors and I could see them clearly. One of them still advises me today and oddly enough I turn to him whenever I have issues over loyalty, proba-

bly because he proved himself so much in that life that I trust him above all others in this.

I learned many things about that life over the course of three regressions. Here I'll highlight the main points rather than give you the whole story.

Soon after my coronation I went to war at the head of my army – and rightly so, it was my place – but when I was away there was an attempt to take my throne by those red-eyed monsters in the crowd, who turned out to be a half-sister and her son who thought my age a barrier to my success.

Having proven myself in battle, I returned just in time to quash their attempt to steal my throne. Not happy, they vowed to seek vengeance and I was urged to deal with them once and for all by putting them to death, which I refused to do. Enough blood had been spilled. It was now time to talk, to find peace rather than another reason to kill people guilty of nothing more than being born in one warlord's kingdom or another.

Over some ten years I toiled to bring the warring factions into line and even though there was more resistance than I would have liked, eventually it happened and peace began to replace war, tolerance to replace hatred, and as I grew older my wife and I ruled over a kingdom built upon those values: peace and tolerance.

Finally I was dispatched into the afterlife by the nephew whose life I had spared. That's karma he has repaid 100 times – and still does to this day as one of my closest friends.

This life taught me that courage is required to overcome adversity and sometimes in life you have to do what's right rather than what you want to do – how do you think this story would have turned out if I had run away? Even though I was out of place at first, I took what was there and worked with it in my own way, one step at a time, and whilst there was many a struggle I never lost sight of my vision. There were those around me who couldn't wait to kill someone and, oddly enough, lived to destroy everything around them, but by introducing the balance of mercy to might eventually they too started to turn things around and managed to smile now and again.

Of course this may come across as idealistic and a little too chocolate box, but why should anyone make an apology for being peaceful, conciliatory or just plain decent? You can be gentle and strong at the same time, and that's the quality this young king had in him. To this day I use his image when I have to go into meetings where I need to have my point heard. It's not quite ruling a kingdom, but then again we're all in charge of our own kingdoms, so maybe it is as valid as ever.

If you need to pull on that power yourself, just take a couple of deep breaths, imagine the person you were and see them in front of you. Then walk into them and put your face where theirs is. Imagine what it would feel like to be them, to have those qualities you so admire, and stand tall. Now go into that meeting with a renewed sense of confidence and know you have been here before, you have learned these lessons and want to simply bring them back to help you in the here and now.

The lack of tears, incidentally, was something that followed me through many lives, causing me to be detached from the reality of my emotions and making things awkward when I couldn't fully express how I felt, but I am happy to say it's being worked on now with someone who expresses their emotions every day and I am glad to return the favour.

The point is not to get caught up in shows of strength for the sake of it. It's inner strength that counts. There are plenty of people out there who will shout at you, call you names and assume they are better than you, but if you're strong within yourself they can never, ever come close to hurting you. That's what a lot of past-life work is about: recognizing your own strength.

Here's a great little exercise for those tough days when you have to find courage and remain balanced between might and mercy.

Before you do this, choose a character either from a former life you have had or someone fictional, someone you admire for their courage (or whatever quality it is you want to bring forward). Just don't choose someone who is alive today in the here and now. OK? Ready?

Find a quiet space. It doesn't matter where it is, as sometimes the need for extra courage comes in the most awkward of places!

Take a deep breath, hold it for the count of ten and then release it.

Do this three times, each time relaxing more and more.

Then imagine you're in a theatre, one with plush red seats and a stage. Be as red and opulent as you like with this one!

See the stage ahead of you and go towards it.

Climb up onto the stage and stand right in the middle.

Above you, you will see a costume. It's the clothing your character would wear. See it in every detail.

As you look it comes closer to you and finally drops onto you and you become that character but with your own face in place of theirs.

Feel those qualities you so admire rushing through your body, making you stronger and more able than ever to deal with whatever you know lies ahead.

When you are ready, open your eyes and go forward with a renewed sense of purpose and strength that will show through and make everyone around you sit up and take notice. Just remember the balance between courage and conscience too.

As well as courage, another aspect of my life as that young king was possessions. There weren't that many then compared to today's glut, but I had more than the average individual at the time and at the point in my life when I first regressed to that life I had nothing of any real value, let alone much money. I am always struck by the saying that we don't possess anything, we only borrow it. Another favourite is 'Do you have possessions or do they possess you?' I think the latter is very true of this modern world where so many people become attached to things as status symbols.

That life made me think about what I had then and what I had at that point in terms of comfort and worldly possessions. I did realize, though, that having more possessions wouldn't necessarily make me any happier, just more comfortable in my misery!

I also recognized that regardless of what I had, by giving away what I didn't want I could make space for other things to come into my life. As I started to do this, I found that if I gave away things that other people thought I should have but that I didn't really want, the effect seemed to double! In my past life I had been told what to do, where to go, when to eat and what to possess, and now I had the freedom to make those decisions myself – how liberating! Clearing out is something you will come across later in the book, and it is also a powerful way to encourage lots of things into your life.

Often, courage in the modern world may not seem like much in comparison with what you had to face in past lives. Times gone by were seemingly tougher, but the truth is a challenge regardless of the time and place and you will have faced many in your lifetimes. What you need to do now is use what you learned.

But sometimes courage and challenge aren't the way to go – what about calm and centred?

CHAPTER 6

PEACE

Thankfully, not all lives are as active, certainly not physically or with such aggression, but don't be deceived into thinking that peaceful lives mean no challenges at all. They are often more emotional or cause us to think ourselves into a hole, to ponder so much that like a swan on the water everything is calm and serene on top, but underneath all hell is breaking loose in an attempt to keep it all going!

This is a perfect example of such a life, and don't worry, I wasn't a swan in it – more like an ugly duckling:

As I landed in this life I could hear someone say, 'Father, wake up. Father, come quickly...'

I was dressed in a robe of grey. It was simple, with a white cord around the waist, and in my hands I still clasped the Bible I had fallen asleep reading. I looked into the face of a novice who was trying to get me to follow him. I knew there was someone on their way to see me, someone of importance who would want me waiting at the door to greet them, and if I wasn't, their mood would not be good. So I hurried, which wasn't easy given that one of my legs seemed to be stiff, almost dead. I dragged it behind me as I walked. 'Pretty,' I thought. 'Yet another fabulously glamorous life for me!'

I made it to the large double doors in time – just. A few seconds later and I would have been in real trouble. A group of horses was coming over the brow of the hill on which the monastery stood. It was warm outside and I had the impression I was in Italy, although for now the century evaded me.

Behind the first group of travel-weary men and horses a splendid figure dressed in heavily embroidered clothing came into view – a man, aged about 40 and very grumpy, by the looks of things. I could just make out some religious symbols on his robes, but my mind's eye wouldn't give me the full information until later. However, I knew that he was in some way senior to me and as part of my faith it was my duty to offer him the highest hospitality I could muster – which wasn't much!

He dismounted and came forward to meet me, then stopped. Where were my manners? I had to go to him and invite him into my humble abode, so I did and kissed the hand he held out before bidding him to follow me.

My monastery was clean. It wasn't hard to keep it that way when there was little in it save for the church and a few wooden beds, a kitchen, an area that looked as though it was for washing clothes and the bathroom facilities for me and the eight other inhabitants, who ranged from another father, older and in retirement, to some monks and a couple of novices. There were fewer novices than of late, a symptom of distraction – there were just so many exciting things to do and see in the world that nobody wanted to stay in a holy order for the rest of their life; and who could blame them?

Back to our guest, who I now realized was from the Vatican and was on a journey at the request of the pope, a journey to show us mere outworkers the glory of Rome and just what we were working tirelessly for. Funny that, I thought I was working for the local people, to bring them solace when they needed it and a place of safety to consider their life and praise the glory of God...

As you may have guessed, I wasn't too impressed with Mr Kiss my Hand. I knew what he could kiss, but it was probably wiser to say nothing. Saying nothing, I showed him to his room, left him and smiled as I thought I caught his nose turn up and his eyes roll in his head at the sight of a single wooden cot, a washstand and not much else!

He was there to ask me how I was doing, so I told him: I had little money, no other resources and more mouths to feed than ever due to a recent illness in the village. God would provide, I was told. I had no doubt about that – God and a lot of hard work from my fellow monks would see us through – but I couldn't help thinking it was the latter rather than the former that was making the real difference!

I smiled diplomatically and got stuck into my chicken, knowing that having it now meant there would be nothing for the weekend, but what else could I feed this great man, so great he arrived with nothing, took everything we had and left? That is what he did the very next day and that is when my inner swan went from serene to hectic underneath...

Matthew was the name of my novice; at least that was the name we gave him. He was bright, articulate and totally devoted to our work, but his devotion to church-going was not as great as it could have been and he constantly missed prayers, although his excuses were always good ones and I wished I had been more like him in my youth. Maybe that was the problem? It was my job to chastise Matthew, to bring him into line and to make sure he obeyed the rules, and I hated doing it. In him I could see a divine light, one that went its own way and should be given every opportunity to do exactly that. The visitor was the catalyst that helped me realize I should be more like Matthew.

Some weeks went by and as they did I withdrew from daily life, spoke rarely and spent many nights in front of the altar, angry, unhappy and repentant, but above all silent. It's silence that brings forward the greatest demons, always was and always will be. But in those quiet times I found I could do battle with them better, I could argue and reason with those inner monsters, beasts created by nothing more than my own imagination and refusal to accept what was truly going on in my heart.

I had had enough, that was the up and down of it. I was walking a path I no longer had faith in. It wasn't that I had lost my faith in my God but in myself. It was time to get it back.

In the dead of night I left. I placed my robe on my bed and dressed in simple clothing. Then I left. It was as simple as that. All those weeks of worry, all those months of chastising myself, and in the end it came down to putting one foot in front of the other and starting a journey without a destination but abundant in excitement.

I moved forward in that life and saw myself happier than I had ever been, with a new home, simply caring and offering spiritual guidance with no rules, only those that were in my heart, listening to those who felt the need to talk, encouraging those who needed courage and smiling every day at bumble bees and butterflies, sunrise and sunset, perfectly placed to watch the world around me come and go about its business.

I died at around 80 years of age, ready to meet my God in the knowledge that I had done my best.

It's not easy living outside the rules, especially when you have been part of the system for so long, but you sometimes have to do it to realize your own strengths and work on those weaknesses. It's all too easy to fall prey to the power and the gifts that come your way for being a good boy or girl and toe-ing the company line, keeping your mouth shut and letting those above you enjoy all the trappings that one day could be yours – but why would you want them? Wouldn't it be better to walk the world with nothing in your pocket and be free than be chauffeur-driven and be at the beck and call of those who hold the strings?

At the time of this regression, I was institutionalized in my own life. I was working for a very large company that specialized in leisure and I was one of their rising stars, put forward to train as a general manager so that one day I could reach the dizzy heights of area manager!

I remember coming back from London one afternoon on a train. I had been to some training thing or other where you sit there nodding off for eight hours and I was on the 4.30 from Waterloo to Portsmouth Harbour – the commuter special. In the carriage there were men and women on their laptops and on their phones, talking shop and calling loved ones on the Isle of Wight, telling them they were on the 4.30 and would be back at seven, as if it was a great thing to be home at 7 p.m! The Isle of Wight to London – daily! What was that about?

Then it struck me: that's where I was heading. I was going to be that person in a few years' time. 'Hello, dear ... yes, on the 4.30. Be home in time to go to bed and get up at six to do it all over again...' No, thanks!

By that time I had had that regression and subsequent ones to gather more information, and I had an idea buzzing around in my head, the idea that I didn't have to be that person, that things had to change. Whilst I admit I am driven as a personality, I do also like to have balance in my life – at least I think I do!

I was back in the office the next day when our own area manager came down on a surprise visit, so bang went my early finish – early was 5 p.m., by the way, and I had been in from 6 a.m. – and we all went and paid court. It reminded me of my regression. There I was waiting for him at the door with our general manager and deputy general manager, the three of us standing there like puppets waiting to have their strings pulled.

Sometime during the day I looked at a corner of the restaurant I was running and there the manager was, pasty-faced, on his laptop, his mobile phone ringing, and I knew he had a three-hour drive ahead of him. There and then I thought, 'No, not for me, thank you very much,' and two months later I was out of there and embarking on my own career.

Did the fact that I had the regression help me to see what was going on? Did my subconscious read the prompts and bring me the opportunity? Who cares, it worked, and I was off doing my own thing, which was where I wanted to be.

Peace comes in many ways in our life. Some people want to be part of a big organization as it offers them the comfort and security you certainly won't have if you work for yourself. For some it's not having any responsibility at all – staying in the same job for years and living for the time away from it. The key is to find *your* peace and to wake up with a smile on your face knowing that you have.

That life also highlighted something those on a spiritual path are usually very good at – giving of themselves – and something many could use a little more of – knowing when to ask for help and to receive it. Where do you need to be more vocal with your needs?

Here's an exercise to help you restore peace in your life. If your own past-life experiences have been about giving up on one route and finding happiness another way, it may also help you to have the courage to take the opportunities that will undoubtedly come your way in this life. Your sub-conscious will bring you the opportunity for change. Take it when you can.

Prepare to meditate.

Imagine you're in your forest. As usual, make sure you are really there. Get into the forest with everything you've got! See the trees, hear the birds, feel the air around you and sense the ground under your feet. Relax and feel safe. Know you're protected and feel happy to be there.

Just ahead you see a clearing in the forest, a space where no trees grow, just an open field. Whilst it looks out of place there's something drawing you to it. Move towards it and stand in the middle of it.

All around you can see your forest. Look at the trees and the path you came in on. There it is – it's easy to spot by the path that you cut through the grass to the middle of your field.

Stand in the field and breathe in the air. It's clear and sharp, clearer than anything else you have ever experienced in your life. It seems to fill you with joy, enthusiasm and happiness, topping up your energy and bringing clarity to your mind and peace to your soul.

Now look up at the beautiful blue sky and see the air as if it's dusted with diamonds. It's full of little sparks of light that seem to dance around you, and as you breathe in they go into your body and fill it with light. They are dancing inside you, making you want to dance along with them, so why don't you? Dance in your field, dance full of the light. Spin around until you're dizzy with all the excitement and fall onto the lush grass, laughing at the foolishness of it all.

Lie there until you get your breath back and then sit up.

Where is your path? At first there's a sense of panic as you don't see your way out, but take another deep breath and remember your intuition led you here and it will lead you back.

Then, as you look around you, you see 100 paths opening up and each one looks as interesting as the next. Which one will you take? Where will it lead you? Does it matter, as long as you're the one making that choice?

You feel lighter than you have ever felt before. Stand up and experience what it feels like to have no burdens, to have only the world under your feet and a path to walk that you and you alone can choose.

Walk towards one of those paths. Go on, just pick one. You will get it right, that you can be sure of.

This path takes you back into your forest, back to the place you started from.

Let the forest melt away, let it drift away and bring your consciousness back into the room. Open your eyes slowly and gently make yourself aware of your surroundings.

Pop the kettle on, get the tea, biscuits, notepad and pen and write down what you saw, how you felt and any great ideas that came to you when you were in your meditation.

Peace comes in many shapes and forms. It's that moment when you fall asleep worry-free, it's the end of the day when you have done everything you had to do, it's the point where you realize something is no good for you and it's time to make a change, and it's making that change. What do you need to change to find peace right now?

☽ ☽ ☽ ☽ ☽ ☽

7

SOUL DETECTIVE

Now it's your turn to have a full past-life regression. Are you ready to find out more about your past lives? I bet you are, but first here are some things to think about. If you're considering having a regression there must have been a trigger, a reason for you to go to all that time and effort, so what was it?

- Do you think you have lived in a certain place before or that a particular person has travelled through several lifetimes with you?

- Do you want to learn where you developed a habit or a phobia that no longer suits you?

- Is there something you want to enhance in your life, perhaps a skill or talent?

- Is your current relationship something you want to look into for whatever reason, maybe to understand why things aren't as they should be or to confirm just what someone really means to you?

- Are your family dynamics less than perfect? Nothing unusual there! I always think it's within families that we learn most of our karmic lessons. You may recognize that delving a little deeper will help – and it will do just that.

Before you proceed, ask specifically what it is you want answering. You won't get those answers all in one go, but remember it's an ongoing process. Here are some questions you might want to ask:

- Why do you feel the way you do about a place or a person? What about those emotions that seem to come from nowhere? What light can be shone on them?

- Are there situations that simply make your blood boil for no reason? Or do you feel strangely linked to another's suffering or joy?

- Is there someone in your life who brings out the best or the worst in you? Do you just want to understand that relationship more or is it that you can't move on from it and would like some clarity, some understanding to help you on your way?

- Are you trying to develop a skill but think you aren't quite making the grade, even though you can feel in your bones that you're meant to be great? Go back and confirm your suspicions!

Preparation

OK, let's start with some basics. Here is how I prepare for a full regression:

- First I clean the room I am going to use. I make sure I do it and nobody else, as this is a sign of devotion to the task I have ahead.

- Then I place a candle in the east, south, west and north of the room I am working in, in that order. Tea lights are best. I place them in appropriate holders somewhere completely safe and then I close the curtains, as natural light shifting and changing in your eyes can be off-putting.

- I burn some incense, maybe frankincense or geranium, and then I put on some beautiful and uplifting music.

- Then I light the candles in the same order as previously described, and as I light them, I ask for the protection of Raphael in the east, Michael in the south, Gabriel in the west and Uriel in the north.

This is the basic formula I use, but you don't have to follow it. Bear in mind this is my way only and you should use whatever methods you feel at home with. A friend of mine lights one candle, rings her singing bowl and walks around the room with it, using the sound to cleanse the room with its magnificent tone. Choose your own way, but once you have decided what it is you're going to do, stick to it. It will become one of those prompts that tells your subconscious you're ready to work and helps it sit up and pay attention.

And one modern thing – switch off all your phones, both landline and mobile!

I also always make sure I am clean and freshly showered before a major regression. It seems only manners when you're going on a journey to talk to your soul. You wouldn't meet an earthly teacher straight out the gym, now, would you?

Some people like to use crystals during a past-life regression, either holding them or putting them around the room. I am one of them – I hold clear quartz and I place amethyst around the room – but they aren't essential. It's entirely up to you. Go with your intuition.

Your first regression

Now make yourself comfortable. As I have said before, it may be a good idea to do this with a friend – a shared experience is so much more valuable – but it's fine to do it on your own.

Please be fresh for this. Don't be worn out or too tired to stay awake – you won't get anything, it will all have been wasted effort and, worse still, it may put you off. People often say to me that they can't meditate, they fall asleep or they can't concentrate, and often it's simply because they are too tired.

Another great tip is, don't be either hungry or over-full. Try to eat about two hours beforehand and you will feel much better for it!

Now sit somewhere comfortable and relax, just breathing in, holding your breath and breathing out. With every breath, imagine your whole body relaxing. Feel calm, safe and ready to listen to your soul.

Imagine that just above your head there is a ball of light, brilliant white light.

Let it sparkle and grow to about the size of an apple and when you have it there, turn your attention to the top of your head.

See a rosebud there. As you observe it, see it open up into full bloom.

Now see a rosebud over your third eye, in the centre of your forehead, and let it open.

Then do the same on your throat.

And on your heart.

Now see the white light that's above your head flowing down through those rosebuds and through your entire body, filling you with white light.

You should now feel brighter, ready to go!

Now in your mind's eye go back to that front door of yours. See it as you did before. Imagine it ahead of you and look at every nook and cranny, every fixture and fitting. Imagine what it would feel like if you were to touch it.

Now see the rest of your house. Look at it in all its detail as if you were standing outside it. See the roof, the walls and windows. Convince yourself you are outside your own house.

Then imagine you're on the roof of your house. Just put yourself up there. You're perfectly safe and secure and content to be there.

Look around you. What can you see? Are there any other houses? Are there gardens and cars or fields and trees? See what you would see from the roof of your building.

Now imagine you are going up into the air — yes, you can fly in this meditation! (But if you're scared of heights, see page 118.)

Raise yourself up about ten yards in the air and see your house from this angle. How different does it look? What can you see in the distance? You can see what's going on further away now: cars in the distance, birds flying by, the tops of trees...

Above you there is a cloud. It's soft, white and fluffy, so why not get onto it? Up you go!

Settle into that cloud, feeling safe and secure, protected and happy to be there. Wrap it around you like a great big duvet.

When you're ready, leave your cloud and go up into
the sky. It's daytime, the sky is blue, the sun is
shining and you're warm and happy.

Take in all the energy from the sun, all the love
and contentment, and let it flood through your
body. See it as a beam of golden light flowing down
through your crown and out through the soles of
your feet, a beam of golden sparkling energy.

Now return to your cloud. Once more wrap it around
you and feel safe, comfortable and protected.

When you're ready, prepare to leave it again. This
time go up into the night sky. The moon is shining
full, the stars are twinkling and it's a cool, crisp
evening.

Take in all the peace and tranquillity of that sky
and let it flow down through your body. See it as a
beam of silver light flowing through your crown and
out through the soles of your feet, filling you with
peaceful and calming energy.

When you are ready, return to your cloud.

Now leave your cloud again and go up once more
into your daytime sky. Once more see the sun, feel
its warmth and let that energy flow down through
your body, but this time push it out of the sides of

your body too. Push it out until you become a ball of that golden energy, full of its love and light.

Return to your cloud when you are ready. Once more feel it around you. Feel safe and secure and know that it's always there waiting for you whenever you need it.

When you're ready, go back up into your night sky. See the moon shining above you. The stars are bright and it's a cool, crisp evening once more. Take all that peace and tranquillity in and let it flow through your body. Then, as with the golden beam, push the silver one sideways out of your body until you become a ball of light.

Now when you are ready, go up further into the sky and keep on going gently upwards until you reach outer space, where you will see Mother Earth beneath you. Stop there.

As you look down, you will see Mother Earth. She is shining there blue, green and white, the jewel of the universe, and she is waiting there for you, waiting for you to return to a former life.

As you observe her, she will slowly start to reverse, to spin backwards. See her doing that and, as she does so, slowly allow yourself to come back down to Earth.

When you think or feel you have landed, look around you. Trust in your images, let them come to you:

- *What are you wearing on your feet?*

- *Are you inside or outside?*

- *Are you male or female?*

- *What age are you?*

- *Are you on your own or is there someone with you?*

- *What are you doing?*

Go with what you see and watch your story unfold... Remember that if you don't like what you see at any time and you don't want to carry on, you can just open your eyes, wiggle your fingers and your toes and bring your consciousness back into the room. Nothing can harm you from your past and nothing can come back with you – you're the one in control.

Into the light

One of the most interesting things about past-life regression isn't always the information you gain from the life, it's what happens afterwards.

At the end of the regression you could find your-self, in fact you *should* find yourself, at the point where you have died and gone into the light. You have to know how the life ended, but don't worry – remember, you don't feel things physically. The best way to explain that one is to think about a time in this life when you broke a bone or had a really bad headache. Think about how you felt. Now are you really feeling the pain or are you just remembering how it felt? It's the same thing with injuries and death in past lives.

So, there you are, regression over and into the light you go... Who's waiting there for you? Often it's someone from that life, someone who needs to give you some more information. Perhaps they need to explain their actions in some way or maybe you have some questions for them. If they are there, there's something to be cleared up.

Don't worry about having a conversation with them; remember, this is your chance to release your fears, let go of anger, accept a gift or bring for-ward a talent, and maybe they hold the key to that.

Endings and beginnings

You have had your regression, you have had your chance to have a conversation with someone who was important to you in that life and now it's nearly time to leave the regression, but there's one more thing you need to do first.

You will have things from that life you no longer need. Maybe it's anger, perhaps it's a tendency to hold on to things when you should let them go, maybe it's a relationship that seems to be repeating itself over the centuries and you are now at the point where it has to be resolved. Whatever it is, at the end of your regression it's time to sort it.

From the safety of the light, see whatever you have to let go of attached to you by a silver thread. It can be colour, a word or a shape, whatever comes to you.

When you are ready, see the thread being cut and just let it go, let it drift off for someone who may need it for their development to pick up. You don't need it any more.

Here's the really important bit: don't turn back and look at it again. Leave it be.

Now you have let go of the negative, what about the positive? What attributes are you really proud of from the life? What do you want to have in your life now, perhaps a skill you had or maybe a way of coping with things? No matter what it is, you have the chance to remind yourself of it and to claim it for your life now.

- *Think about what you want to bring for-ward.*

- *See it as a light or energy and imagine you're wrapped up in it.*

- *Accept it into your aura, your own personal energy.*

Now see those energy points you opened up at the beginning of the regression closing: at your heart, your throat, your third eye and finally your crown.

When you are ready, open your eyes, wiggle your fingers and your toes and bring your consciousness back into the room.

Time for tea and biscuits. Record your life and what happened in the light within the next couple of days. Also, it's really important to let in any additional information that comes through. Write it all down – your subconscious won't stop talking to you just because you're not meditating.

An alternative

If you have a fear of heights and it isn't going to fill you with excitement to rise up into the air even in your imagination, here's an alternative visualization to help you explore your past lives. Even if you're OK with heights you might like it better or find it easier to remember. Any way you want to use it is fine by me!

Prepare the room and use the same opening procedure as before.

Imagine you're in a forest. See it in your mind's eye in as much detail as you can. Feel the ground under your feet, see the trees, smell the foliage, listen to the animals around you... Is it warm or cold? What trees and plants are around you?

See a path ahead of you. Follow it through your forest. It's perfectly safe and an easy path to walk along. Keep following it until you reach a clearing.

In the clearing you will see a massive tree and at the base of that tree there is a large door made of silver. As you look at it, magically it opens...

Go through the doorway. Ahead of you is a room with a black-and-white-chequered floor and that floor is strewn with herbs that release their fragrance as you walk over them. Smell them. What do you smell?

Ahead of you is an altar covered with a simple white cloth. Burning in the centre of it is a single blue flame. Behind that altar are two pillars and between those pillars is another doorway. Again it's silver – the metal of memory.

Move towards this door and as you do so, ask in your mind for a life that's appropriate for you at this time.

As you approach the door it opens, so walk through it.

You seem to be lifted up. Is it water, is it air, is it angels' wings? As long as you feel yourself being lifted up, that's up to you. Just go with what you feel comfortable with.

Eventually you will find yourself outside a magnificent silver temple. This temple is in the shape of a pagoda. It is waiting there for you to enter.

Move inside the temple and towards the altar, where you will see several lamps, oil lamps like the one Aladdin found his genie in, but there's something more precious about these lamps than a genie. One of them will help you find a past life.

You will know which lamp to choose. Trust in your intuition and pick up this lamp of memory.

Carrying this lamp, move towards another door behind yet another two pillars.

As you do so, the door opens. It seems to be filled with a mist, a mist filled with a brilliant white light. Move towards it and walk into it...

Keep walking, keep walking, and as the mist clears, be aware of the scenery around you. Have a look at the landscape. Where are you?

Start with your feet. What are you wearing on your feet? Are you male or female?

Now follow on as with the other regression technique.

Afterwards remember to close down and ground yourself effectively.

Now how do you feel?

As if you have been on a very long journey and could use a lie-down, no doubt, but was it an adventure?

How many questions do you have now? I bet there are loads, depending on what you saw, of course, and how you saw it. Remember, if you got very little, that doesn't matter, you will still have questions, and answers will be provided if you put the effort in.

If you feel the regression has brought up some things you would like to have some help with, then seek that help. This is no time to go it on your own because you think you have to – nothing could be further from the truth. If you want professional help and don't know where to go, there are some ideas at the back of this book, but often a supportive friend interested in the same sorts of things is all you need. If you have been doing the regression together with a friend, though, do remember the words 'trust' and 'respect' and don't go talking about their past lives inappropriately.

On a physical level, remember you may be exhausted, so take some time to rest and recuperate and have a little princess sleep if that's what you want. Sometimes the tea and biscuits will be enough to revive you, but on other occasions it's chocolate brownies and ice cream all round!

Of course, you may want to take some action based on what you saw. Remember the techniques in this book that are designed to help you remove any blockages you may have and to bring whatever you need from the past into your life now. It doesn't matter if the life you have experienced bears no resemblance to the issues in your life now – the techniques are universal and should be used whenever you feel they are appropriate.

The greatest help of all will be physical action. No matter how small the step, take it! Sign up for that course you have always felt drawn to. Maybe it's learning a language you have already spoken, so will have a natural gift for, or perhaps it's something wonderfully creative that will help you express yourself more. Whatever it is, use it and don't lose it again!

I have seen many people come for past-life work and after one session never come back, not because they didn't enjoy it or get something out of it but because they just got wrapped up in the life they were living now and all that it brought them and often spent all their time struggling against the tide in order to just stay afloat. Odd, isn't it, when you're thrown a lifeline, to just look at it and throw it back and set off swimming against the tide again...

CHAPTER 8

SILENCE AND CONTEMPLATION

Let's have a look at another type of life. You won't have had the same lives as me, but you will have shared some of these experiences, just in different ways, and by looking at some common themes, hopefully we can help each other see the purpose behind them.

You would think a life lived in silence or without much human company would deliver very little in the way of lessons. Sure, you would learn how to be happy on your own, content to get on with things. It would be a case of, in the words of my Royal Navy report from this life, 'Works well without supervision', but would there be anything else? What do you think...?

I found out for myself once, though I didn't exactly plan to. There's not much you can do to control where you arrive in past-life regression when you first start, though later you do have some of a say, but this life was early on when I was content just to see what was out there.

I thought at first that I had landed in ancient Egypt at last, but then I realized it wasn't Egypt at all. There were no pyramids, only sand, and some odd headdresses rather than the full Aida treatment. Egypt was still eluding me.

I was in Syria or Persia. I couldn't make up my mind which, but I was in a temple and I was offering what seemed like entrails to a god whose face was obscured, as if I wasn't allowed to see it, but his feet were golden and his legs were black. I was female, about 16, and I knew I had been training in this place for years, although what I had been training for wasn't going to be revealed just yet.

I finished my ritual and walked into a side room where I disrobed and threw the bloody garment I had been wearing to one side, bathed in a very ritualistic way, starting specifically with my feet for some reason, and then put on a clean linen robe.

I walked into a room with a bed and some very fine food and drink, drank some wine, lay down and slept. I was in a past-life regression, that I knew, but then I started dreaming as well. That was odd and a new experience for me. I was dreaming of swords falling and helmets clashing. Shields were being raised and one was very memorable as it had a snake on it. Later I drew it before I forgot what it looked like. The dreams were changeable, but always there seemed to be a war theme and surely in that life I wasn't warlike at all...?

I went forward in that life and found myself in front of a king, a very grand king. I was describing my dreams to him and his generals, and then it struck me – the wine, it had been drugged to encourage me to see, to see as in 'seer'. That was one of my roles: to predict the future for this king and his court.

That regression was one of the haziest I have ever had. I couldn't see as I usually did and couldn't hear as I usually did. Perhaps it was the drugs I was being given – without my knowledge, I am sure. I thought the visions were coming from myself. It seemed

I had had psychic gifts as a child and had been left at the doors of the temple. After that, as is the way with some people, my power had been controlled and used.

Then one day the doors to the temple were opened and I could see two very large men entering the room. They wrapped me up in a sheet and carried me out without a struggle, which I thought unusual.

I was placed into a set of rooms which were comfortable and as I looked around I realized something – other than speaking to the king and uttering some words in the temple I hadn't ever spoken to anybody. Then a realization came to me: I was to be an oracle, a seer who would pass on information in return for food and lodging. My work for the king now over. I had been replaced by another favourite, retired at about 24 to serve whomsoever wanted to come to me.

Locked in, I sat and communed inwards and learned to love the silence. I recognized the power of it. It was the very thing that people built my mysticism on. It made me different in their eyes, but the truth of the matter was it was I who saw them as differ-ent – unattached to the source, too busy wondering if their business would fail, if love would return or some seemingly mun-dane issue would resolve itself.

Having had enough of it all by the time I was 30, I left this world disillusioned, but the truth is I was too detached. Overdoing silence is a misuse of its power; there is a difference between silence and inertia. I could have done something to break free from my gilded cage and used my gifts at my own discretion rather than in response to others' demands, but I drowned in the sea of my own silence.

At that time in my life the unfolding wisdom of the Qabalah was pressing down on me and I knew I had to change things within a very diffi-cult relationship, one where the person involved wasn't showing me any respect. Whilst I knew there were faults on both sides, I wasn't willing or able to talk things through, preferring silence, hiding behind my office door and losing myself in my work, on some occasions coming out only to eat.

Silence is power – it gives you the upper hand because nobody knows what you are thinking or what you will do next – but usually the truth is we are silent because we don't want to do anything or we fear change. On this occasion it was the negative side of the past life which was influencing me, making me go towards silence rather than speaking out, so that habit had to be broken, but the power of silence still had to be adhered to – not an easy thing to do. If I had used it wisely, I would have retreated, thought things through and kept the person waiting for my decision. Then, when I was sure of it myself, I would have said my piece. Instead, I said my piece only to myself, over and over again, and the silence became a sanctuary I couldn't leave until one day it got too much and at the worst possible time, my birthday in fact, I had enough and handled things badly.

Lessons were learned, and what the past-life regression had shown me was just how I had had the power at first and then handed it over as an easy option. And then, when silence consumes you, you don't want to share anything with anyone. You want to keep even misery to yourself. If I had only given it up, given birth to a new idea or a different way of life in my past life or in the real-life reflection of my past existence, things would have been a whole lot different – 'different', notice, not 'better' or 'worse'. Regret isn't the point; dealing with things as they happen is.

Here's something you can do if you feel too detached, too away from it all, and are yearning for a fresh beginning:

- In complete silence go up to your bedroom, open your wardrobe door and sort your clothes into 'Hang on to', 'Give to charity' and 'Chuck out'.

- Then do just that, without saying a word – just bag them up and chuck them out. (Don't tell anyone you live with you're going to do this, by the way, otherwise they will think you've really lost it! Just say you don't want to be disturbed.)

- As you put each thing into the 'Chuck out' or 'Give to charity' pile, attach an emotion or an experience to it, something you don't want any more – things from being too picky over who does the washing-up right through to arguments over nothing and ignoring the real issues. Then imagine it leaving your life as you get rid of the garment. (Don't worry about passing these emotions on to anyone who buys your clothes in the charity shop, by the way – that won't happen!)

- Now, as you restock your wardrobe, think of all the things you do right. Sort out your clothes and as you handle each garment think, 'I am a good laugh' or 'I love my kids' or 'I walk the dog every day' or 'I provide for the whole family' – whatever you want. Do it that way round and by the time you finish you will feel lighter, want to communicate more and realize that hanging on to things isn't the best way to go.

If you feel you need a little more, here's a meditation:

See yourself in your forest. You are comfortable and safe, secure in this happy place.

As you begin to form your usual scene, let the sound of the sea drift slowly across your inner hearing.

Take your normal path into the forest, but this time as you approach your special tree you will see a sign that says 'To the Beach'! Walk that way instead of going to your magical tree.

Almost as soon as you make the turn, things begin to change. The sky opens up as the trees and plants of the forest disappear and you can feel the warmth of the sun on your face and hear the sea sounding ever closer.

Now the ground begins to change. Patches of sand start to appear and slowly but surely those turn into a beach, a long golden beach, a cove with nobody there but you.

The sea is magnificent, as calm and as blue as it can be, with a gentle swell that's almost hypnotic. Stay a while and watch it.

When you're ready, go further along the beach.

As you walk along, you see a cave. It's lined with crystals. Are there any you feel drawn to?

Walk into the cave. Feel safe and secure in this womb-like space and sit down.

Meditate in this sacred space and this time let your subconscious mind put in the route. Let your soul speak.

In that silence wait for answers to appear, for new ideas to form. Wait to give birth to your own brighter future, all the time absorbing energy from those crystal walls and strength from your silence.

When you are ready, and only when you are ready, make your way back along the beach.

As you reach the end of the cove, look back. What do you see? In the distance there is your own soul, silent but communicating with you from that centred and powerful silence. It is with you whenever you need to commune with your higher being.

Now walk away from your beach. See clumps of grass and fern begin to replace the sand as you move once more into your forest and back along the path you came on.

When you are ready, let the forest disappear and bring your consciousness back into the room.

Tea, biscuits and journal – you know what to do.

Red cars

If I told you about a red car, if you had a red car, if all you saw for the next ten minutes was pictures of red cars, then the moment you went out of your front door you would see more of them. You would think there had been an increase in the number of red cars in the world, but the truth would be you were simply more aware of them because you had been feeding your subconscious with that image.

Imagine then what you could do if you were to spend some time in silence thinking about what you wanted in your life. If you were sitting there reinforcing an image of success, of happiness, of healthy eating, of new love in your life, what then? As with the red cars, you would go out and see opportunities to succeed wherever you were – but would you take them?

That's where silence and contemplation come in. They supply you with the ability to withdraw for as long as it takes to think things through, to meditate and to project those images out into the universe so that when you're ready you can grab them!

When past lives show themselves to us it's clear we have to rely on our inner self, that part of us that knows the answers to our questions, but we often ignore it simply because life gets in the way, it seems too difficult, there's not enough time, or any other excuse you can come up with! But the purpose of doing past-life work is always to benefit you in some way in this life, never forget that. It's there to show you solutions, and sometimes silence is the key.

When this life as an oracle showed itself to me I was as busy as ever, but I didn't think that I was too busy to ignore my inner self. I was, though, and it took the regression to wake me up to the fact that I was caught in a similar cycle, so focused on one thing that I had actually cut myself off from all the possibilities around me and, just as in my previous existence, I was doing what was expected of me rather than what I really wanted to do.

Once you recognize a pattern you have two choices: you can go with it and put a smile on your face or you can stop and start a new one. It's not easy, nobody would argue with that, but once you get used to being more observant, to using quiet times to commune with your own inner oracle and, of course, to taking action as a result of what you find, you will achieve so much more.

CHAPTER 9

SUDDEN CHANGE

Life can be surprising sometimes. Often it can shift in a second, whilst sometimes things drag on forever. We all suffer from it – one minute we are chugging along doing this, that or the other, and then along comes an event that shifts everything in the blink of an eye. But surely that's about this life and not the past? Well, yes, but maybe the things that are happening today are echoes from the past. Wouldn't it be worth taking the time to get creative and have a look?

And what about those slow, slow times? Maybe a past-life regression is what you need to open up your creativity, get those ideas flowing and get excited about things?

Using your new-found skills to keep things moving is essential. All too often people associate past-life regression with solving problems, which it can do, of course, but what about creating positive outcomes, opening up new doorways?

Here's an example.

Life seemed to have stood still for Gareth. He was doing OK, but OK wasn't really good enough and even though he was happy enough he didn't feel as if he was doing what he really should. But when asked what he wanted to do, he always said, 'I dunno.'

Having a regression was an idea that came out over dinner one night when he thought he would ask me a million questions instead of eating his meal. I eventually turned things around and asked him what he did for a living and he told me all about life in a bank. Well, coffee couldn't come quickly enough! But seriously, we had the 'dunno' answer when I asked what he really wanted to do and it's then that I suggested a past-life regression might help. It was certainly worth a go.

Here's what happened.

Gareth was nervous, never having done anything like this before, but I reassured him, he brought a friend with him for support and we got on with it:

DW: Just tell me when you think, feel or know you have landed.

G: OK, I think I am there.

DW: Where?

G: I can see a mountain with snow on it.

DW: Do you know which country you are in?

G: Not yet. I am just breathing in the air. It's so crisp, so beautiful.

DW: Take your time.

G: I think it's Italy. I am near the Alps.

DW: What year is it?

G: Early 1900s.

DW: What's your name?

G: It's too corny for words!

DW: Go on.

G: Antonio.

DW: So you're male, and it isn't corny!

G: Is this real or am I making it up?

DW: Go with it. You can rationalize things later.

G: OK. This is so weird...

DW: What's happening now?

G: I can see a woman. She is about 24. I'm around 27.

DW: Go on.

G: She is my girlfriend, I just know she is. She is smiling at me. We are going to marry, but I am unhappy. (He cries at this point.)

DW: What's wrong?

G: She is going to die, I just know it.

DW: Go on.

G: We are going to a small house. It's her parents' house. It all seems so ideal, but there is this cloud hanging over us.

DW: What is it?

G: She is ill.

DW: With what?

G: Nobody knows. She is just so ill, some days she doesn't get out of bed, and I sit by her, holding her hand as she sleeps. I love her so much.

(Now I cry.)

DW: Carry on, let's see what happens.

G: She dies one day. The sun is so bright, the air so fresh and yet she is gone, gone, and I can't get her back. I am distraught. (He cries again and this time I step back and let him cry and cry, releasing the pain he has held back for centuries.)

DW: Do you want to continue?

G: Yes.

DW: What's happening now?

G: There are children, lots of them, and they are sad. I think she was their teacher.

DW: Where are you?

G: I am playing with some of them in a playground. I am happier when I am around them.

DW: Why?

G: It's their innocence. They just get on with it and every day is an adventure.

DW: Do you recognize any of the children from this life?

G: One of them looks like my girlfriend.

DW: OK, now let's move on to much later. Where are you?

G: I am on my deathbed. I am not that old, but I have a wife and three children of my own.

DW: What's happening now?

G: I have died. My heart gave in.

DW: Can you see the light?

G: I can.

DW: Go towards it, Gareth, let it surround you and let me know when you have done that.

G: OK, I am in it.

DW: From the light, can you tell me what it is you would like to let go from that life?

G: The pain of losing her. I think it still affects me in this life, I think I may be too clingy with relationships.

DW: See it as an object or a word and now see it attached to your belly button by a silver thread. Now see that thread snap and let those emotions go, let them drift off where someone else can pick them up to help them with their soul growth. Once you have let them go, don't look back.

G: Done that.

DW: Now what do you want to hang on to from that life?

G: The joy, the joy of just being in the moment with those kids.

DW: See that joy as a colour and wrap it around you. See yourself surrounded in it and when you want to have that feeling again, just wear that colour.

G: Done that.

DW: Well done. When you're ready, open your eyes and bring your consciousness back into the room.

(There was a lot more information in this 45-minute regression, but for expediency and Gareth's privacy it has been edited.)

So what happened next? Hands up, who thinks Gareth now runs a ski-school for kids in the Alps? You'd be wrong! We did some more work together, though, and Gareth explored his options carefully. Then suddenly he made his move. He left the bank and went to work for a charity organization working with children, and his girlfriend (now wife, I believe) went too. He went off using not just his very analytical brain but wearing the biggest, brightest smile I have ever seen. 'I dunno' had turned into 'Now I know!'

There is no doubt in my mind that we are here to create, not just in the procreation sense of the word, but to make something from nothing, to move things forward, to help life go on and progress, but above all creating makes us happy.

When was the last time you started a new project, thought about what it was you really wanted to do with your life or maybe just picked up a paintbrush and let your talents show on canvas? It doesn't really matter what you create, it's the smile on your face when you can step back and say 'I did that' that is important.

CHAPTER 10

MAGICAL OR MYTHICAL?

There are sometimes lives that seem too magical to have ever existed. Lives in Atlantis are one such example – how could they ever have been real? What if I told you that not only have I been regressed to this time but I have also done many regressions for other people who have described the same harbour, the same system and the same downfall and have never met each other in this life?

Once I was giving a lecture in a health spa and at the end a young woman came up to me and told me she didn't want to ask me a question, she just wanted to say hello to a fellow Atlantean. I had had my Atlantis regression by then, but it still freaked me out as she looked into my eyes and I saw it all being reflected back from hers.

Here's my version of events:

The harbour was shaped like the letter 'U' with two magnificent crystal obelisks acting as a gateway to a city that shone in the sunlight. The city was pure white, the sea bluer than sapphire and a gentle hum seemed to come from it, as if it was alive.

I found myself in a garden. I was old, very old, and was tending the plants under my care, mainly exotic flowers by the looks of things. I was very tall and wore a robe of purple and on my forehead there was a crystal, which kind I wasn't sure, but it seemed to be purple in colour too and I knew it wasn't an amethyst.

I moved forward and found myself in a chamber containing a mighty crystal, one that seemed to have moving images inside it like a giant hologram, and as I moved closer to it I could hear a voice coming from it. I recognized it instantly. The woman speaking was one who has travelled with me through many lifetimes and now she was on our sister island of Lemuria, which was odd, I thought, as it was usually men who lived on Lemuria. Where did that come from?

She told me to beware, she felt things weren't right and there was going to be an uprising. She asked me to do what I could to quell it.

'Like what?' I asked.

'Whatever you can,' came the reply, so I asked to meet those people who lived lower down the hill.

Atlantis was built on a hillside and there were three classes. First there were some odd-looking men and women who were almost like cavemen in their appearance. They could communicate perfectly well, but were devoid of any scientific or artistic skills, or so it seemed. Then there were the middle races who were teachers and builders, doers, the type who just got on with life and spent what little time they had spare mainly teasing those lower down the hill or hounding those higher up – which was where I stood. Here were the scientists, poets and artists. We were tall and hardly spoke, at least with our mouths. We were telepathic and had a connection that ran between us all. We had been sent to help the *middle and lower levels learn and grow, to attain better things for themselves, but somewhere along the line it had all gone wrong...*

Now they were beating the doors of our temples, demanding our information and our crystals and killing our kind. Blood was being spilt on Atlantis, which filled me with dread. I tried to reason with those I knew, those who came to my classes on crystals and energy, those whom I thought I could trust, but they all had red in their eyes and I knew we were lost.

They tried to get to the crystal room and as they approached I beat them to it, locking myself in. I communed with those who were watching us and a decision was made: destroy the link, break the crystal. The experiment was over. And so I did – not alone, mind you, there were many of in that room and it had to be a unanimous decision, which it was.

We focused our energy on the crystal. It wasn't long before it cracked and Atlantis was no more, with Lemuria following. It rained and rained and rained – nothing unusual there, you might think, but we had never had rain before, our water had always come from the ground. I was astonished to see rain.

Some people got into boats, but most of us perished and that included me, drowned along with thousands of others.

Success

We all want to be successful in life, to do well and to have what we want, regardless of what those goals are. We measure our success ourselves, or at least we should, but the truth is we often associate success with how others see us or what we own.

In achievement, as in everything else, there has to be a balance. That balance is keeping a sense of reality around you. Unfortunately, there are too many examples of those who think they are so successful that dreaming up silly things to prove just how great they are becomes a habit – flying bottled water around the world to have in their hotel suites or only drinking tea hand-picked by monks, for example. Wake up and smell it!

When I tell my very successful and well-grounded teacher about some of the people I come across, she sometimes says they must be spiritually poor if they behave like that. For a while I wasn't sure what she meant and as usual it bothered me and bothered me until it cleared. Finally I realized what she meant was if you're spiritually wealthy you don't need such physical props. You don't have to have people fawning over you to sustain the illusion that you are a success, because your own spirituality feeds and sustains you.

Of course, this doesn't mean you have to live in a hair shirt and meditate every morning before popping off to work at your local charity shop. You can have a great car, a beautiful home or a yacht in the South of France if that's what you want – the trick is to enjoy it and of course share it.

At the time when the Atlantean life came to show itself I was at a point in my Qabalah training where I thought I had discovered the answer to everything in the universe and as such was a force to be reckoned with – the big I am, as we say in Scotland. Of course, the reality was completely different and for once it only took a PLR to wake me up rather than for a great big brick wall to fall on my head, so I did actually learn a lesson without having to repeat it in this life.

To this day I celebrate when I have a success that feels good to me, but I always try to put my hand back and help others. The danger is, the more you advance, the less you do it, but I have found a way through the wonders of the Internet and hopefully through writing.

Devotion

There is a danger that anything you do, whether or not it's about your spirituality, becomes all-consuming and whilst you're busy thinking you're doing things for the good of others you are in fact doing them for yourself. So how do you ground yourself and become devoted to what you do while remaining devoted to who you are?

One way is to remain aware of *where* you are. As one higher arc on your path comes close to fruition you begin on the lower arc of another; in other words, you come to the end of one cycle and you begin another. Your past-life work will bring all sorts of cycles into your life. Truth is, they were always there, but now you should become a lot more aware of them, and keeping track of them all is important if you're to proceed to new and exciting things.

To help you, here's a little catch-up, a consolidation of what you could have learned so far:

- *My key life is:*
- *My central life is:*
- *My inner bully was:*
- *I have brought back this:*
- *I have left this behind me:*
- *This person travels with me:*
- *This is what they show me:*
- *The theme in my lives so far is:*
- *I would like to revisit this life:*
- *I need to know more about:*
- *I would like to heal this:*

📖

Go through this list carefully and truthfully and add any more points you can think of.

It's worth doing this exercise every year, which may sound like a long time, but when you look at how many years you have been reincarnating here on Earth, it's probably a drop in the ocean!

Past-life investigator

HAVING A CLUE

We have already established that writing things down is the way to go, but what do you do with that information? And is there anything else you can do to help you remember your past lives or to validate them? Of course there is, or why would I have mentioned it?

You may be happy to accept the information you get as it is, but some people won't be, so get as much out of your regression as you can. You can tape your sessions if you're with a therapist or even if you're doing them with a friend. In fact you can even do it on your own if you don't mind talking to yourself – even if it is your former self!

If you can get clear information during your regression, try to find out the following:

Names – yours and those of the people around you.

Location – what country, what county, what area, which street?

Dates – an obvious one, really, but so many people forget it! It's not just the date you land, by the way – try to find out when you might have got married, when any children might have been born, when you died... All are relevant and could provide proof.

Fashions – a great indication of time period if you're struggling with dates. What are you and others around you wearing?

History – who's on the throne, what's the name of the president, what's the food like? Make a note of anything that could give a clue to where or who you are.

Make sure your notes are thorough, trust in your intuition when more information comes through afterwards and don't forget to draw any images you get – emblems, flags, buckles, anything you think could be useful. Another great idea is to draw a map, perhaps of your village or street or maybe just a rough plan of the layout of your house from a former life. It's all important stuff when it comes to looking for proof or looking back for a link between lives.

Imagine if you were to actually go and visit a site where you once stood hundreds of years ago, somewhere you had never been in this life but you were holding a valid map to the area right there in your hand. What more proof would you need?

Something else worth recording is the 'Eureka!' moment. That's the moment when the light goes on in your head and you make the link between your past life and your present and what that means to you going forward. There will be several, and seeing them written down in black and white makes them real, something you can touch and recognize as growth in both your spiritual and physical life.

This will also help you determine where you would like to go next. Will it be on to another life or is there more to be gained from going back to that one? Once you have experienced a life, you can revisit it as and when you feel the need. Just set your intention before you begin your meditation.

What about personal relationships? Do you have more to uncover that could help with your relationships right now? If you feel a certain life has something more to give you, revisit that life. Leave no stone unturned. Be as creative as you want to be and remember this is a tool that can be used for your growth in any way you see fit.

If you do decide to go back into a life you have already experienced, it's a good thing to read through your notes beforehand to remind yourself of why you're going back and just what happened the first time round. I wouldn't recommend you go back too soon – give it a couple of months so that you can process the information you have received to date.

Even if you don't get much second time round, still write down what you do get. It may seem like nothing now, but further down the line it could be very important indeed, and struggling to recall something isn't a situation you want to find yourself in.

Timeline: making some changes

This simple technique will help you reprogramme your subconscious to see another way of dealing with anything you don't like from a certain life. It will also have a knock-on effect in this. It's a great way to change attitudes and patterns – and not just yours!

When you are in a life you will recognize a point where everything took a course for the better or worse. If it's the former, then well done, you, but sometimes you will wish you had done things differently, so now's your chance!

Imagine going back and fixing things, getting right what you think you have done wrong, sorting out a relationship that wasn't handled the proper way or just taking back what you said. You may not be able to do it in this life, so what about the last one or the one before that?

Think of one of the lives that's having an impact on your existence right now. Pick something you did in that life, something you wish you hadn't. Read your notes from that life, remind yourself what happened and then prepare to go back into it.

This time when you set off, ask for that life.

When you get it, go through it swiftly in case you missed anything and then go straight into that glorious safe and secure light at the end when you die.

From that safety, look down on your life as if it were a movie and when you see the point where things went pear-shaped, stop it. Just push 'pause' and hold it right there.

Now drop back into the life at the that point and relive it, but this time make your changes and see what happens and just how differently things turn out.

Finish your regression in the usual manner.

Once more write out what you get and keep it safe.

This isn't only about making you feel better, which I hope it does, it's about changing any interpersonal relationships you may have in your current life by changing what happened in your past.

If it all sounds a little too much, think about it again. You're sending a message to your subconscious that says you don't want these conditions any more, you're making some changes and you expect changes to happen here and now in this life. It's surprising just how this works and even if it's only a shift in attitude from someone who previously wouldn't give you the time of day, then doesn't that show you something?

Flipping the coin

Heads you win, tails you still win! What if instead of waiting for a past life to show itself that would explain the karmic conditions that are impacting on your current life, you did things the other way round?

Say you're having relationship issues, family problems maybe – do they come from a past life and would accessing it take you some way towards solving things? Maybe you don't know what to do on the work front and you would like some guidance or perhaps you would like to develop a skill you're sure you used to have?

Whilst you can never guarantee you will get the life you want, you can rest assured that if you make a solemn request before your regression and hold the intent as you go into it, the chances are that you will get some information that will help you.

You really do need to be clear about what you are looking for, though – any wishy-washy requests will be met with an equally watery regression where nothing much is gained. Remember that with meditation and visualization, intention is everything.

In my own life I was once experiencing difficult times letting go of a relationship that just wouldn't pale into that place where the ex lives, that 'happy to have known you but time to move on' place. I asked to see the life that had set up our karmic conditions and was shown a life where I was dependent on this soul for everything – but of course things are different now and I make my own way in life now. The memory was holding me back. Once I saw myself as a strong, independent and happy being, I could let this pattern go, and as soon as I did, the usual happened: I saw my ex and thought, 'What was I doing?' Off they went to ex land...

CHAPTER 11

CAN YOU MOVE FORWARD IN TIME?

Surely if you can move backwards in time, you can move forwards…? And what about that space in between lives? It's an interesting thought…

Here's James's story. James was a young man who had a reclusive side to his nature. He could sometimes withdraw for weeks on end and his friends would just let him get on with it, knowing he would come round when he felt like it, but those who didn't know him that well would give up on him early on. It was surprising he had any friends at all, really!

Here's an account of his regression:

DW: Tell me when you have landed, James.

JH: OK, I have landed.

DW: What are you wearing on your feet?

JH: Nothing. They are bare and cold.

DW: Why are they cold?

JH: They just are.

DW: OK, now can you tell me if you're male or female?

JH: Male.

DW: Age?

JH: About 34.

DW: Are you inside or outside?

JH: Outside, looking at a house.

DW: Is this your house?

JH: No.

DW: Who owns it?

JH: I don't know, but I am going to live in it.

DW: How do you know that?

JH: I just do.

DW: OK, James, can you see yourself in the house and tell me what you see?

JH: It's very nice.

DW: Do you know what date it is?

JH: Late 1800s.

DW: Can you be more specific?

JH: No. Why are you asking all these questions? (James becomes confrontational at this point.)

DW: I am trying to find out more about your life.

(James smiles, but it isn't a comfortable smile – more threatening than anything else.)

DW: Are you OK, James?

JH: I'm fine. How are you?

DW: I am fine, thank you for asking. What's your name in this life, James?

JH: John.

DW: John what?

JH: Just John.

DW: What are you doing now?

JH: Just looking around the house. Seems nice. I think I could live here.

DW: Are you thinking of buying it?

JH: No, just living here.

DW: Are there other people around?

JH: Yes, I can see a couple of children.

DW: Are they your children?

JH: No.

DW: Whose are they?

JH: The people's who live here, I guess.

(At this point I am asked by my own guides to help James move to a mirror so that he can see his face.)

DW: James, can you move towards the wall on your left, where you will find a mirror. When you do, can you look into it and tell me what you look like?

(James gasps in horror.)

JH: I have no skin! My face is half-skeletal and the flesh is coming off my hands!

DW: Remember you are perfectly safe, James. Just go with what you see. If you would feel more comfortable, move away from the mirror.

JH: OK.

DW: Why do you think you look like that, James?

JH: I am dead.

DW: So why are you here in this house?

JH: I am haunting it. I don't want to move into the light.

DW: Why would that be, James?

JH: I wasn't a very nice man. I did terrible things.

DW: What did you do?

JH: I murdered and robbed people. Now I don't want to go to hell, so I will just stay here. It's much better.

DW: You won't go to hell, James. You only judge yourself.

JH: So you say!

DW: Can you tell me more about your life before this point?

JH: No, I'm ashamed.

DW: It's OK. I want to understand.

JH: I was a robber. I stole at first, then murdered for money.

DW: So you were a sort of mercenary?

JH: If you like.

DW: How did you meet your end?

JH: I was bludgeoned to death near here. Under a tree is where my body lies now.

DW: So you know where you are buried?

JH: Yes.

DW: Which county are you in, James?

JH: I don't know. (He begins to get upset and wants to move on.)

DW: OK, James, I want you to do me a favour.

JH: What?

DW: Go back to your tree and see the moment you were killed. You don't have to feel any pain, just tell me what happens.

JH: There are four of them. They are setting about me with shovels and their fists. I don't stand a chance. I recognize one of them. I think I murdered his father. This is my comeuppance.

DW: Do you think you deserved it, James?

JH: In a way, yes, I do.

DW: James, can you see the light?

JH: I told you I didn't want to go into it.

DW: But can you see it?

JH: Yes.

DW: Are you sure you don't want to go into it?

JH: Yes, I know what happens. I will go to hell.

DW: How sure are you about that?

JH: Sure.

DW: Can you see anyone in the light, James?

JH: Yes, I can now. I didn't see her before.

DW: Who is it?

JH: My mum. (He cries at this point.)

DW: What is she saying, James?

JH: That it's OK, I won't go to hell. I will have to answer for my actions to myself and that will be hard enough.

DW: Do you trust her?

JH: She's my mum.

DW: So what are you going to do?

JH: I don't know, I don't know, I don't know...

DW: It's up to you, James, but think of all the healing you can gain if you move forward now.

JH: I know.

DW: So...?

JH: I will go into the light. Can you come with me?

DW: Of course. Just imagine me beside you if it helps.

JH: OK, I am in it.

DW: Surround yourself with that light, James, see nothing but the light, and tell me when you have done it.

JH: OK. I feel at peace, I feel happy, I feel brighter.

DW: Is there anyone in the light, James?

JH: The people who murdered me.

DW: What are they saying?

JH: They are asking me for forgiveness, but I am asking them for the same thing.

DW: What's the answer, James?

JH: Love.

DW: It always is and always will be.

JH: I am exhausted.

DW: Do you want to leave this life?

JH: Yes.

DW: First, James, what do you want to let go of?

JH: (Laughs) That's not hard to figure out – regret, foolishness, anger, pain, everything associated with this character.

DW: See it attached to you by a silver thread. Now let it go and don't look at it again.

JH: OK.

DW: What do you want to bring forward from that life?

JH: Strength – not physical strength, but the courage to do the right thing.

DW: Are you happy to leave it there?

JH: I am, very happy.

This was an extraordinary regression for me to witness. James had been haunting a house, but he had done it in the complete knowledge that he was doing it! This was something that was to be of even more interest later in my own life when I went on to do a television show about ghosts!

As for James, we did a lot more work on this life and others, and eventually he felt the need to withdraw lessen. He became brighter in himself as he learned to forgive himself and to take charge of his life, to walk in the light instead of hide away in the darkness.

James also went back to find out why he had turned out to be such a difficult character in that life. He got his answers and began changing the outcome, which had a knock-on effect on the present – of course.

This was a reminder to me that no matter how odd, magical or mythical a regression appears to be, it's always good to stick with it. You can doubt and dissect it when you have all the information, so try not to push the 'pause' button too soon.

James didn't end up in his view of hell, but if your regression takes you to a place that's suspiciously like your interpretation of heaven, go with it, I say! There's a lot of information to be gained from seeing what goes on in the astral worlds and some people do go there, although I am not one of them – at least not in past-life regressions, anyway!

If you do find yourself in the spiritual realms, the information you gain will be limited. It's been my experience, however, that people who do go there come back with a sense of great peace and calm, which has to be worth it in this modern world!

Tomorrow's World

So, if you can go back and if you can go between, you must be able to go into the future, right? It's an interesting thought and it can happen, but it's been my experience that these lives are given rather than asked for. In other words, you may be interested and you could ask, but you won't automatically get them.

Going into the future – progression – is not something I have done consciously, but I have done it at the end of a regression by simply going with what I was given. It wasn't so much forced on me as suggested I paid attention. I won't go into what I saw here. Suffice to say it wasn't unpleasant, but it was a real eye-opener.

I have never offered progression as a technique, but it is something I am asked about a lot and as such it clearly deserves to be talked about. So what is it?

There are two ways of looking at it: will your progression be about possible outcomes in this life or future lives? The fundamental question I would have is this: how can you benefit in the here and now from that information? That's the real point of it all.

If you really want to do it, here's a word of warning: *do not* have a progression on your own. Seek professional help from someone qualified in this technique. Why? Self-fulfilling prophecy – you will tend to put all your energy into what you see happening and along the way you will forget about what you're supposed to be learning. You will miss out, because in your curiosity you'll be hurrying things along when there really is no need.

So why bother? Well, some people just really want to do it. And if you're going to do something, you're going to do it. Do have a plan, though, and do it only under professional supervision.

If you really want to know what's coming up for you, maybe a visit to your trusted astrologer, clairvoyant or Tarot reader would give you just as much guidance?

And talking of astrology...

))))))

CHAPTER 12

PAST LIVES AND ASTROLOGY

Please try not to read this section until you have done at least two regressions of your own, whether prior to reading this book or as a result of it. The reasoning behind this request is very simple: if you have the regressions before you read what your astrology says and there is some sort of confirmation in what you find, you will have another layer of proof, another reason to believe in what you have seen. If you check your astrology first, though, you might go into a regression with preconceived ideas and miss out on something vital.

Suns and doubters

We all know what astrological sign we are and we are usually well aware of the blessings and challenges of that sign, but sun-sign astrology, the kind found in magazines and newspapers, has no relevance to your past lives. You have to look a little more closely for that, but you can start with something as simple as your sun sign – star sign, if you like.

But before you do, first think about why astrology might exist. Surely there would be little point in such a complicated thing as your astrological birth chart unless you had lived before? Why would you have such a set-up if you only incarnated once? Reincarnation is therefore a given in astrology and your chart is there to show you what you have already learned to do well and where there is room for improvement.

So let's take a look at the sun signs. If you have read my first book, *David Wells' Complete Guide to Developing your Psychic Skills*, you will know some of this information already. If you haven't, I have repeated it so you don't feel left out, and to be fair, even if you have read it before, this updated version could bring you some new insights into your sun sign and past lives.

So what influence does your sun sign have on your life? Say you're an Aries, that makes you a little noisy and usually ready for a fight if the circumstances allow, but where does that attitude come from, is it just because you're an Aries or have you nurtured your confrontational skills throughout the centuries? And are you supposed to be enhancing them or finding another way to deal with things?

Some people believe your sun sign gives you some idea of the age of your soul, with Aries as the youngest and Pisces as the oldest. This isn't something I would subscribe to, as I know lots of very wise Aries with ancient souls and some skittish Pisces with very young souls. A discussion of soul age is for another time; suffice to say, you can have had hundreds of lives and learned nothing or you can have had few lives but have struggled and learned huge amounts. There are no hard and fast rules and, as any astrologer will tell you, your natal or birth chart shows just how unique you are.

Flipping the wheel

The zodiac is made up of 12 signs and most people know them, but which one is your opposite number?

- *Aries opposes Libra.*

- *Taurus opposes Scorpio.*

- *Gemini opposes Sagittarius.*

- *Cancer opposes Capricorn.*

- *Leo opposes Aquarius.*

- *Virgo opposes Pisces.*

So what? Well, if I tell you that your sun sign shows a lot about where you left your last life, it doesn't take too much to consider that your opposite number is what you're aiming for in this incarnation. That might give you some idea of the lessons you could concentrate on in your past-life work as you try to bring about balance.

ARIES–LIBRA

If you were born under one of these signs you really are on a mission to maintain balance and to enhance your understanding of relationships, especially those that are up-close and personal. The Aries part brings leadership and the ability to get things moving, whilst the Libra part shows it's all right to take a step back and think things through. Again, balance is the key, but if you're Aries you will rush at things and if you're Libra you will dither about. Find the midpoint!

In past lives this arc could have brought lives of solitude, times when you had to be on your own for one reason or another and had to do things for yourself, and that can sometimes leave you prone to walking away from a relationship rather than working it out.

Aries will show great impatience and a need to have things done now if not sooner, and of course done their way, whilst Libra will go over the top to help others but will call that favour in when they feel hard done by.

Give and take is the karmic lesson here. Being able to see when that's being tested will help, as will the regressions you have that concern those one-on-one relationships. Just use the information you receive to sort them out! You're striving to find perfection in relationships, but that's not the real aim, which is why you may fail. The true aim is the simplest, and that's give and take. That's what maintains balance – the constant ebb and flow.

TAURUS–SCORPIO

How you equate your possessions with your spirituality, that's the balancing act for this configuration. What do you have to give up in order to gain in either area?

Money is usually a big lesson for this set-up and that could have come from lives where it came to you all too easily or you failed to learn its value.

Having a goal, a dream, is usually a high priority for you and in order to reach that, sometimes you feel as if you have sold out, doing something just for the cash rather than because it's what you truly want to do. Does the end justify the means?

In previous lives you're likely to have been part of a wealthy family or had your needs met in some other way, but in this one you will have to work for your keep, make no mistake, and all without losing sight of your ultimate goal.

There is also a tendency with this arc to like to eat, drink and sleep a lot, so you're battling with energy, with getting your get-up-and-go going, but once you find the right goal, nothing can stop you. It's usually about playing the long game, taking time to build strong foundations and learning how to move things along within your comfort zone and to keep on moving!

GEMINI–SAGITTARIUS

Your head's all over the place running with great idea after great idea but failing to get anywhere through being inconsistent, remaining the enthusiastic child and refusing to grow up and accept full responsibility for your actions. 'Jack of all trades and master of none' comes to mind and with this challenging balancing act it's not easy to delve deeper and ensure a job's well done rather than half done.

In past lives it's likely that you didn't have to make many choices, that things were put in front of you. For some this could mean many lives in a monastic situation where everything was controlled.

Sitting around thinking of what you would do if this, that or the other were different is a classic reaction with this arc, but it can be broken and that's why you need to find the lives that matter. By understanding your need to be flexible and to have more than one thing going on to keep your interest, you can have success, but don't expect it to be in one field. Play the field – play many, many fields! Choose a profession that constantly teaches you and forces you to learn things day to day. That way you will feed your flexible soul whilst encouraging growth through your true panacea: knowledge.

CANCER–CAPRICORN

Cancer is the sign of motherhood and whilst there is certainly nothing wrong in displaying strong family links, inherent in this arc is also the need to be successful and to be seen as being a success.

This arc also displays itself differently between the sexes. Cancer is mother, Capricorn is father, so if you're a Cancer male you may come across as being over-emotional and if you're a Capricorn female people may mistake ambition for coldness and hardness, particularly at work. Neither is true, but the archetype of home life versus career is very strong with this configuration and you could find it has karmic repercussions as you have to constantly make choices based around those very things. There is no right and wrong and it's entirely up to you how you deal with this, but remember that balance is what you're aiming for.

The reason why some of your past lives come to you may be to show that there is room for both home and career. An absence of family and/or career in a former life could also explain why the desire to polarize in this one exists. The trick, then, is to find a way to have both.

LEO–AQUARIUS

Bright sunny creatures with bags of personality and a desire to be in the spotlight, you guys are all front – particularly you, Leo! 'Why?' is the question on everyone's lips! Maybe you have had past lives where you were doing anything but being in the spotlight, working away in the background, making it better for everyone else and taking none of the credit – well, now things are different and look out, world, because here you come!

Often those with this arc don't take to being told what to do that well, believing they could do their boss's job better than them and being willing to give it a go, given half a chance! Creativity is usually very high here and you can rest assured you will have a solution that nobody else will have thought of – and that's where your real strength lies.

Balance is also key here. Leo needs to learn to lead but to serve those who look up to them, and Aquarius should bear in mind that being part of a group means just that: 'part of' not 'better than'.

VIRGO–PISCES

If you're a Virgo it's about details and you will have honed your perception through many past lives, and if you're a Pisces that perception could move between worlds. This is a highly spiritual arc. You have both experienced most things and you may find that when you do past-life work you jump from warrior lives to religious ones to family ones and back via all roads in between, but there is likely to be one common thread in all of them and that's your spirituality.

Applying yourself to some sort of learning on a spiritual path could benefit you a lot and no matter which one you choose you can rest assured you will do well, because you are likely to have studied it before. So is it to be Buddhism, Qabalah, Zen...? Whatever, it doesn't matter as long as you follow that path with precision!

You should also always keep your eyes firmly fixed on what's to come, as dwelling on the past could lead you into a melancholic frame of mind, hoping for the good old days that won't come back. Even though your past-life work *is* going backwards of sorts, it's meant to push you towards greater things in this incarnation.

Your worry and concern over what might happen are born from many lives where things went wrong in order for lessons to be learned. But you have learned them and, more importantly, you have learned *from* them. You won't repeat them once you recognize what they are.

The nodes of the moon

In my last book the north nodes of the moon were introduced to give you some clues about what you're aiming for in this life. The north node's running mate, the south node, will give you some clues to your past lives and the types of lessons you may be dealing with. When coupled with the sun-sign information above, it can open your eyes to quite a few things. Don't worry, this isn't technical stuff, and when you put the two together your own subconscious will be only too quick to let you know what the combination means for you!

A node, by the way, isn't a planet, it's a point formed in this case by the moon's orbit around the Earth and where it intersects with the Earth's path around the sun. Got that? Don't worry, the chart at the back of the book will tell you where your south node is and all you have to do is find it, read it and put it alongside your sun-sign information.

I have also included an affirmation for each sign to help you draw on the gifts from your past lives. An affirmation is something you say to yourself about 20 times in the morning and 20 times at night. Not forever and ever, just until your subconscious gets the message and helps bring change about. It's not complicated – try it!

ARIES SOUTH NODE

In past lives you are likely to have been a warrior, fierce in your approach to people. On occasion you may have alienated some of them, simply because getting too close was only going to result in loss, so why bother?

Acting swiftly and without thinking, you may still rush into things without thinking them through, and learning how to co-exist in a relationship of equals could be a challenge for you, but will hold great rewards if you can master it.

Fight against a desire to be the centre of attention. You have had enough of that, albeit through waving a sword in people's general direction! This time it's about other people and their needs. The chance to love is what this current incarnation could be all about and your node in this position could bring lots of relationships your way. The trick is to learn to cherish them and learn from your other half.

You have probably learned to make decisions swiftly, but try to remember that others may well need more time, and even though in previous lives you often got your way, the same may not be true now.

Like all good warriors, you need discipline. You need to know where the boundaries are and what rules need to be followed, which means setting them up early in any relationship, be it professional or personal.

Affirmation:
What I have, I share, and when I share,
I get ten times more returned.

TAURUS SOUTH NODE

Dealing with money or having issues about your physical wellbeing could have been your lessons from a former life. And weight issues or making the most of your innate ability to get things done, albeit slowly, are probably high on the list of things for you to address now.

You're likely to have been creative in your former lives, with the senses playing a major part. Think dressmaker, potter, painter or cook. Now you're likely to be set in your ways and have a very clear idea of what has to happen for you to be happy, and you can carry a lot of baggage as a consequence. Seeking approval from others by doing the right thing can also be prevalent. This is born of lives where routines had to be followed to the letter, say in a religious ceremony or ritual.

No stranger to comfort in a past life, you may overindulge in food and drink, but in this life those indulgences may not be appropriate and are likely to cause a problem with things like weight and even the pursuit of luxury at the expense of values.

Listening to the input of others is crucial to bring a freshness into your current life. Failure to do so could see you set in your ways, learning nothing much and repeating old cycles – and yes, I *am* saying you can be stubborn!

Money karma is high with this node and learning to let it flow rather than hoard it could be a major lesson. Just how you go about that could take a past-life regression or two to unlock...

Affirmation:

When I do nothing, nothing is what I get in return. In order to have something I am doing something.

GEMINI SOUTH NODE

Letting go and trusting in your intuition are crucial for you; if you over-think things, you will only tie yourself up in knots.

In past lives you are likely to have been in a position where you had to know what others were thinking – maybe a teacher, writer or other communicator of some sort – but you were all too concerned with other people, so now it's time to think about yourself and what's true for you. Putting things across in another's language isn't putting *your* point across and you need to learn to speak your own truth rather than trying to fit in with that of your peers.

You may be tempted to ask everyone around you for their opinion, not once but 100 times, and even when they give it to you, you ask again, and again. But what you have to do is trust in your own self rather than be influenced by the approval of others. Once you learn to do that, you will take what you have gained in your past lives and turn it into something that will work really well for you.

You're likely to have been surrounded by people in your past lives, but in this life you will need to seek silence in order to work things out – and if that's not an excuse for a spa break, I don't know what is.

Affirmation:
When I trust in what I feel, I connect with the universe and all is well.

CANCER SOUTH NODE

Family, tribe, clan – whatever you called your gathering, you're likely to have been at the heart of it, and that's where you're likely to want to stay, but what would that teach you? You must now learn to step outside, to embrace the big wide world and be master of your own destiny, in charge of your future.

Family karma is likely to be strong here, which simply means those you have travelled with in past lives are likely to be members of your family (that's true for many of us, but more so for Cancer south node) and therefore you won't have to look far to learn lessons!

Putting your life on hold until the kids leave school, Mum remarries, Dad's hip replacement takes place or the dog's worming treatment is successful can be excuses for simply not getting on with things, and learning that there is room for it all in your life is important.

Control is something you may have to temper, to give up if you can, and the sooner you realize you are neither in control nor responsible for everything, the better.

One thing that's always prevalent with past-life work is that the most beneficial course of action is the toughest. It's tough because you have spent lifetimes setting up habits and cycles and now it's time to break them. For Cancer south node the hardest part is stepping out of the front door rather than staying in just in case somebody needs them. *Life* needs you, so get out and meet it!

Affirmation:

I am supportive of others, but responsible only for myself.

LEO SOUTH NODE

Being special is something you would have come to terms with in past lives, perhaps as royalty or an entertainer of some sort, but most definitely as someone in the spotlight, which means of course you may find it a bit odd now the light has gone out and you're left to learn that things happen to all of us and it's that shared human experience you have to participate in.

Having had a VIPL (Very Important Past Life), you could take it to heart when people don't let you have your own way now. Forget the pout, it won't work. What *will* work is involvement with the team, so get stuck in.

Bear in mind, by the way, that you're unlikely to be a good loser – in fact, any form of gambling is to be avoided, as, let's face it, you're going to lose at some point, so why put yourself through it?

One thing to remember is to be sure of what you want in life. If you focus your attention hard enough, you can have pretty much anything, but getting what you *don't* want is all too easy, as you may be going for glamour rather than the truth of who you are. Make sure you sort that one out first.

Your first instinct in this life may be to go it alone, but that worked way back when you were the ruler and everyone did your bidding! Now it's about teamwork, and the sooner you realize that, the better. Use the leadership learned from past lives, but use it with humility and an idea of what's needed for the common good.

Affirmation:
I am important, but I am no more or less important
than anyone else.

VIRGO SOUTH NODE

Doctor, nurse, healer – regardless of culture or method, you were the one people turned to and you had to get it right every time. Rules and regulations had to be followed and things done one way or not at all. If the rules were broken there would be worry and turmoil.

Holy orders as a monk or a nun could also have been part of your past-life tapestry and people would have looked to you for guidance, but these lives could have brought detachment from the practical realities of people's lives.

Analysing everything is a tough act to maintain all of the time and learning to trust in your intuition a little more would do you the world of good. Worrying about what could happen is also a waste of time and you might be wiser concerning yourself with what *is* happening before wasting any energy on the woulda, shoulda, coulda.

Your greatest gift in this life could be your ability to bring order where others fail to even come close, but it has to be applied gently. If you go in with 'Must do this', 'Won't do that' and 'What do you think you're doing?' nobody will listen. Be gentle and firm but fair.

Criticism is something you may not like. Guess what? You're likely to get more than most in order to learn that other people's judgements aren't as important as your own and their criticism is a way for you to move forward rather than stand still and worry about it!

Affirmation:
All is well. I am in the right place at the right time.

LIBRA SOUTH NODE

You were more than likely the power behind the throne in your past lives, the one who supported others and gave them the energy to further their careers or ambitions. But don't think this was a selfless act – it was to keep yourself out of the limelight and ensure your own survival.

The problem with giving so much for another is the possible loss of your own identity and it may be that which keeps coming up as a theme in this life. You may well have to concentrate your efforts there.

You probably mirror other people really easily. Watch what you do during conversations – do you copy the gestures of those you're talking to?

You will have lots of love to give, but woe betide anyone who crosses you, because you will take only so much and when you flip, you really flip!

You need harmony and peace in this life to function properly, but don't mistake that for failing to say your piece. The challenge you could face is to become more of a warrior than a peacemaker when circumstances require it.

Coming to a decision over an important issue may not be easy, and it's harder still if it's just you who has to make the call. You don't do so well on your own, having had so many incarnations as part of a team, so guess what, you're likely to be challenged on that one!

Affirmation:
My opinion matters greatly. I am having my say.

SCORPIO SOUTH NODE

The one who set things up, saw where to go and directed people in the right direction, queen to a powerful king, general in battle or perhaps a wise woman of the village, a life immersed in the magic of the Earth, that's your past-life profile!

Being provided for was highly likely and whether that was as a consequence of your power or because you exchanged your healing gifts for food, things came to you with ease. That, of course, means you have to work harder than anyone in this incarnation!

Power struggles were also highly possible, which may have left you with a confrontational mindset, preferring to raise your voice first and think diplomacy later – mainly far too late!

Your inner bully is stronger than most, so re-read that section and reinforce the visualization to release any hold-ups that could cause.

You need to have a comfort zone, a happy place, somewhere you feel secure and are able to let go of all the frustrations of modern life. Get a massage, book in for a spa weekend, make sure you have a garden – anything except eat your way out of a moody!

A strong loving relationship – and a highly physical one at that – will really help you feel that sense of security. Soul mates are strong with this node. You will know them when you see them.

Affirmation:

Nature is nurture. I will return to her when I need comfort.

SAGITTARIUS SOUTH NODE

Seeking the truth, past incarnations as pilgrims, nomads, travellers and mountain-top hermits may have been yours, which is why in this incarnation you love to travel, and very often on your own. These past lives could have left you with a superiority complex, or at least the appearance of one, and you may have your work cut out convincing those around you to listen to your ideas. Listening is as great a part of communication as talking – two ears, one mouth, a combination made to pay attention to what others have to say.

You may also see the bigger picture and forge ahead into the future but fail to think about how you are to get there. Paying attention to detail is important and it could be a lesson you have to learn in both your private and professional life.

In your youth you may have stuttered, trying to get too much out at once, but as time goes on you realize that by taking your time, things sort themselves out. Think about what that means. Could it be that getting out as many words as you could was more important than what you said – in other words, you were looking at quantity, not quality?

Always ask for clarity if you don't understand anything, as there could be a tendency to let things slide too. Do that and you will end up in trouble.

You are here to teach, to give others the benefit of your ability to hold on to knowledge – knowledge that has been gained through lifetimes of experience.

Affirmation:

When I slow down, I understand more. I have time.

CAPRICORN SOUTH NODE

In past lives you're likely to have had incarnations where normal family life either wasn't to be or was absolutely everything! Both extremes are likely, with little in the middle ground.

Respect is important to us all, but more so to you. You are used to being the boss, the one everyone looks up to, but are you entitled to that or do you have to earn it? You know the answer to that one!

Success is important to you, but it's likely to be driven by the need to be on top rather than the desire for financial gain. That's very nice, but it isn't what makes you tick. You're here to regain your connection with the rest of the world, and the family is your number-one starting point. That's not as easy as you might think, as I am sure you have already found out!

You're dependable and will keep your word; all you ask is that others do the same. You may be very disappointed when they don't.

You could feel responsible for everything and everyone, but the truth is you're not. Once you learn that and truly let go and let others grow, you will find life gets easier all round.

You're probably goal-orientated and will do well when you set yourself targets. Organize your life as if it were all business. This doesn't sound romantic, but organization is key for you. But that does mean organizing without assuming control and responsibility for everything in the whole wide world!

Affirmation:
I benefit when others take charge of their own lives.

AQUARIUS SOUTH NODE

Past lives as scientists, observers, watchers looking at things through microscopes and in macro climates, not getting involved in things – guess what the balancing act here is? You have to engage, have fun for the sake of fun and set your inner child free. If you don't know what or who your inner child is, there are many great books on the subject. Read one and be surprised at just how much fun you can have!

Creativity is also key for you. Take up painting and drawing if you like, but making something from nothing is the real deal, starting your own business.

You could also benefit from being in the spotlight, the centre of attention. A great antidote to all those scientific lives could be as an entertainer. Give 'em the old razzle-dazzle!

In the world of spirituality, you're particularly connected to the angelic realms and may very well find that angel therapy works well for you.

Taking risks is also something you may be challenged on. The more you invest in your creativity, the more risks you may have to take, of course, but play safe and you probably won't advance as quickly as you otherwise could.

If in doubt, think about approaching things as a child. Children have no fear, they are naturally creative and they know how to have fun!

Affirmation:
When I release my inner child, I win every time.

PISCES SOUTH NODE

Hold on to your ego, here's the list of past lives this node can indicate: lives spent in meditation, spiritual quests, drug or alcohol abuse, asylums and prisons, as well as in writing poetry and making movies. A wide range there! But ego is in fact the last thing on your mind. When I said, 'Hold on to it,' I could just as easily have said, 'Try and find it,' for you are the least egotistical of the nodal signs.

Giving up too easily could be a hangover from your past lives – it was easier to give in than fight on, and not having any ego meant that many things weren't that relevant any more, so why bother?

Having been shut away from society on many occasions, you need to learn how to adapt to the real world, to be where you should be when you should be there and to have a schedule you can stick to.

Your imagination is likely to be incredible and using it would suit you well: think film-making, writing scripts and of course visualization... I suspect you're very good at the exercises in this book.

Learn to eat well to ground yourself and to say 'no' when you feel something isn't right for you, as you are likely to have temptation put in your way often and it's part of this life's lesson to resist it.

Order and routine are your friends – the more of them you have in your life, the easier it will be to deal with things. A great barometer to how you're doing is to have a look at your home – is it tidy and neat, or is it messy and all over the place? When things are going well, the former is evident; when you may need to get things together, you will notice your living space is untidy.

Affirmation:

I am the one who can sort this. I am a winner, not a victim.

So that's the nodes. Hopefully they will have given you a greater insight into where you have come from and some idea as to where you could be going next.

Now combine your node with your sun sign. Look at both and write in your journal your impression of what this means. Don't forget to let anything intuitive come through – when you do this you will be surprised at some of the illuminations you can get. For example, I am a Gemini with a Pisces south node. Although the Gemini–Sagittarius arc coupled with the Pisces node means I have had lives where I have been kept away from people, it's clear that in order to offset that karma I have a life where I am very much in the public eye. I need order and routine in my life to make it work and I constantly have to be learning something new as well as sharing my knowledge. My past lives have helped me to raise my spiritual energy, but now I have to be more practical in its application. Even though I work with these conditions every day, I am sometimes lost in the mists of my Pisces south node, but I recognize it and bring myself back to Earth through good food and giving my creative side an outlet through my writing.

There's more there, but you get the idea. Be fluent with it, let it flow!

CHAPTER 13

WHAT NOW?

So you have done your past-life regressions, you have selected some that are more relevant than others and you have thought about things along the way – what now?

You won't stop investigating, you will go on using the information you have gathered to date and you can look forward to all those exciting things you still have to learn. It's a never-ending feast. Just be sure you use what you have learned. To help you, here's a recap:

You are the result of your past lives. All the people you have been, the places you have seen and the experiences you have had have equipped you to deal with your current incarnation and to clear your karma without creating too much for the next time round!

Your past-life work will have led you to identify patterns, and once you know what they are, see where they have come from and understand where they are heading if they aren't tackled, you will want to clear them and start better ones.

The connection between your personality, your soul and your spirit will be clearer and they will all be able to fulfil their true purpose rather than have their lines of communication blocked by centuries of negative emotion and regret.

You have a tool that won't just bring you past-life information but can also help you to connect to your guides and angels when you need them.

A new perspective can be gained from looking at your current life from your past and vice versa. Where do they have common ground and just what do you want to let go of and to hang on to?

Life will get in the way of your development, it always does, but now you have tools to help resolve those issues a lot more swiftly, and when you apply them, situations that would have caused you sleepless nights in the past no longer take up your valuable time.

When faced with repeat situations from your past, you will recognize them instantly and immediately know what to do to clear them – replay the tape and remember what not to do and what has to be done.

Your belief system will be strengthened and your independence within that system will be heightened. You will recognize that you can be as creative as you want, no matter what deity, faith or religion you subscribe to.

Your 'Eureka!' moments will be easier to recognize and when they come you will make a note to look a little further into whatever has brought them about, whether a new relationship, a new place to live or a new situation you find yourself in. When you do, your intuition will be confirmed and what you find will help you move forward.

You will use your magical image, have a word with that inner bully or recognize the resonance of your key life in everyday situations, but above all your soul will shine through, and when it does, magic will happen!

As ever, your spiritual development is in your hands and only you can take it forward, but I hope you now have another tool that will help you do so. Remember, it's about the practical application of your magical gifts. Don't be so heavenly minded you're no earthly good. Too much wafting about and not enough housekeeping will get you nowhere fast.

Use your gifts wisely and when you see me, tell me all about it.

Now, where are those biscuits?

☽ ☽ ☽ ☽ ☽ ☽

LOCATING THE NODES OF THE MOON

Your south node is listed according to your birth date:

9 Mar. 1935–14 Sept. 1936	Cancer
15 Sept. 1936–3 Mar. 1938	Gemini
4 Mar. 1938–12 Sept. 1939	Taurus
13 Sept. 1939–24 May 1941	Aries
25 May 1941–21 Nov. 1942	Pisces
22 Nov. 1942–11 May 1944	Aquarius
12 May 1944–3 Dec. 1945	Capricorn
4 Dec. 1945–2 Aug. 1947	Sagittarius
3 Aug. 1947–26 Jan. 1949	Scorpio
27 Jan. 1949–26 Jul. 1950	Libra
27 Jul. 1950–28 Mar. 1952	Virgo
29 Mar. 1952–9 Oct. 1953	Leo
10 Oct. 1953–2 Apr. 1955	Cancer

3 Apr. 1955–4 Oct. 1956	Gemini
5 Oct. 1956–16 Jun. 1958	Taurus
17 Jun. 1958–15 Dec. 1959	Aries
16 Dec. 1959–10 Jun. 1961	Pisces
11 Jun. 1961–23 Dec. 1962	Aquarius
24 Dec. 1962–25 Aug. 1964	Capricorn
26 Aug. 1964–19 Feb. 1966	Sagittarius
20 Feb. 1966–19 Aug. 1967	Scorpio
20 Aug. 1967–19 Apr. 1969	Libra
20 Apr. 1969–2 Nov. 1970	Virgo
3 Nov. 1970–27 Apr. 1972	Leo
28 Apr. 1972–27 Oct. 1973	Cancer
28 Oct. 1973–9 Jul. 1975	Gemini
10 Jul. 1975–7 Jan. 1977	Taurus
8 Jan. 1977–5 Jul. 1978	Aries
6 Jul. 1978–5 Jan. 1980	Pisces
6 Jan. 1980–24 Sept. 1981	Aquarius
25 Sept. 1981–16 Mar. 1983	Capricorn
17 Mar. 1983–11 Sept. 1984	Sagittarius
12 Sept. 1984–6 Apr. 1986	Scorpio
7 Apr. 1986–2 Dec. 1987	Libra
3 Dec. 1987–22 May 1989	Virgo
23 May. 1989–18 Nov. 1990	Leo
19 Nov. 1990–1 Aug. 1992	Cancer
2 Aug. 1992–1 Feb. 1994	Gemini
2 Feb. 1994–31 Jul. 1995	Taurus
1 Aug. 1995–25 Jan. 1997	Aries
26 Jan. 1997–20 Oct. 1998	Pisces

21 Oct. 1998–9 Apr. 2000	Aquarius
10 Apr. 2000–13 Oct. 2001	Capricorn
14 Oct. 2001–14 Apr. 2003	Sagittarius
15 Apr. 2003–26 Dec. 2004	Scorpio
27 Dec. 2004–22 Jun. 2006	Libra
23 Jun. 2006–18 Dec. 2007	Virgo
19 Dec. 2007–21 Aug. 2009	Leo
22 Aug. 2009–3 Mar. 2011	Cancer
4 Mar. 2011–29 Aug. 2012	Gemini
30 Aug. 2012–18 Feb. 2014	Taurus
19 Feb. 2014–11 Nov. 2015	Aries
12 Nov. 2015–9 May 2017	Pisces
10 May 2017–6 Nov. 2018	Aquarius
7 Nov. 2018–4 May 2020	Capricorn
5 May 2020–18 Jan. 2022	Sagittarius

READING AND RESOURCES

Aristia for books, crystals – you name it, they have it, and all delivered to your door:

Aristia
233 Albert Road
Southsea
Portsmouth
PO4 0JR
United Kingdom

Tel: +44(0)23 92355645
www.aristia.co.uk

❧❧❧❧❧

My teacher's website: www.orderofthewhitelion.com. You'll find the answer there. Now what was the question?

Need a therapist?

The Past Life Therapists' Association
Hypnotherapy South West
Virginstow Beaworthy
Devon
EX21 5EA
United Kingdom

Tel: +44 (0)1409 211559
www.pastliferegression.co.uk

Titles of Related Interest

Ask Your Guides, *by Sonia Choquette*

Life-Changing Messages, *by Gordon Smith*

Daily Guidance from Your Angels,
by Doreen Virtue

Archangels and Ascended Master Cards,
by Doreen Virtue

Feel Happy Now, *by Michael Neill*

Ask and It Is Given, *by Esther and Jerry Hicks*

The Law of Attraction, *by Esther and Jerry Hicks*

Angel Numbers, *by Doreen Virtue*

Angels Watching Over Me, *by Jacky Newcomb*

Notes